NAFC
Members' Cookbook

Edited by
Mike Vail

North American Fishing Club
Minnetonka, Minnesota

Acknowledgements

We would like to thank the following for their help:

NAFC Members, for sending us those delicious, original wild game recipes that serve as the foundation of the 1996 NAFC Members' Cookbook. These recipes – recommended by your fellow NAFC Members – are certain to delight.

NAFC staff members, for their diligence, patience and hard work in seeing to the preparation of a useful and readable cookbook of which the NAFC's Members can be proud. They include Marketing Manager of Books Cal Franklin and Project Coordinator Amy Nielsen.

Lawry's Foods, for their delicious fish recipe contributions.

Lou Bignami, outdoor writer and cook extroardinaire, for parting with some of his favorite fish recipes.

Book Design and illustrations
by Zins Design Studio

Please address reprint requests
and orders for additional cookbooks to:
NAFC Cookbook Editor
P.O. Box 3401
Minnetonka, MN 55343

ISBN 0-914697-66-8

Dedication

After all these years of producing our popular <u>NAFC Members' Cookbook</u>, we've failed to recognize one particular group for its contribution to the success of this annual publication: The NAFC Staff.

You won't find a more dedicated bunch of anglers anywhere! We put in long hours to create the Club's great magazine — *North American Fisherman.* We also spend a lot of time working to provide Members with all the benefits they deserve and look forward to, the benefits of membership in America's leading fishing organization.

Every year, as we start work on the annual Members' Cookbook, we read through hundreds of recipes that are sent to us by Members of the Club. And it's a tough job to separate the best so they can be included— they all sound so good.

This year, as we were sorting through Member recipes, a thought struck us: what about all the tried-and-true recipes enjoyed by our own Fishing Club staff? Who would have better recipes? After all, even though we spend a lot of time taking care of Club business, most of us somehow find time to get out on the water in the quest of our favorite gamefish.

So, I sent out a memo. Each staff member was asked for his or her favorite fish recipe. And we got a bunch. In this edition of the <u>NAFC Members' Cookbook</u>, you'll find some of our favorites.

This edition is dedicated to the Club staff, without whom this would all be impossible.

Mike Vail,
Editor

Contents

Cookbook Abbreviations

tsp. = teaspoon
T. = tablespoon
pt. = pint
oz. = ounce
pkg. = package
qt. = quart

Measurement Conversions

1 pinch = less than $\frac{1}{8}$ tsp.
1 T. = 3 tsp.
2 T. = 1 oz.
4 T. = $\frac{1}{4}$ cup
5 T + 1 tsp. = $\frac{1}{3}$ cup
8 T. = $\frac{1}{2}$ cup
16 T. = 1 cup

1 cup = 8 oz.
1 pint = 16 oz.
1 quart = 32 oz.
1 gallon = 128 oz.

1 cup = $\frac{1}{2}$ pint
2 cups = 1 pint
4 cups = 1 quart
2 pints = 1 quart
4 pints = $\frac{1}{2}$ gallon
8 pints = 1 gallon
4 quarts = 1 gallon
8 gallons = 1 bushel

Introduction

From Our Kitchen to Yours—

Top Recipes of NAFC Members & Staff

Crackling, the fire began to burn down, leaving only coals glowing brightly in the stiff wind blowing off Reindeer Lake. George, our guide, wasted no time. He leveled a grate over a few rocks scavenged from the shoreline and rested a huge, smoke-blackened frying pan on it. Another shorelunch was about to begin.

George waited until the potatoes were almost done before he started frying the fish—small pike and walleyes we'd caught just minutes before. Then, he gave the signal and everyone crowded around with plates in hand. The fixin's weren't fancy, but on that cold northern Canadian afternoon, it was a meal topped by no other.

I was well into my second helping when I noticed George was still cooking, but not fish or potatoes or beans. In front of him sat a bubbling can of Spaghetti O's—and a fork.

George explained between mouthfuls. After more than 30 years of guiding, he had eaten more shorelunches than he would care to admit, and frankly, he was tired of fried fish (and potatoes!).

Couldn't blame him.

I appreciate that George is truly a hater of fried fish. Not that I agree with his assessment, mind you, but he does serve as a great reminder that there are more than just one way to cook fish, all of them delicious.

The recipes you find in this book are supplied by NAFC Members and staff. Many of them have been in the family for years, and are shared now because nothing brings folks together better than a good meal.

Yes, you will find fried fish recipes in here. One of them is mine and it's a good one. Easy, too. Just don't use canola oil. Learned that one the hard way.

Other great recipes to check out include:

- Beth Metzen, head of the Member Services Department, offers two ways to cook salmon. One is a stew, the other a loaf.

- Forrest Fox, Associate Producer of NAFC videos and avid angler, shares his favorite way to cook pike—on the grill.

- Jay McNaughton, of the Member Products Department, spent six straight weeks one summer in the Boundary Waters Canoe Area of northern Minnesota, where he learned several ways to cook fish. His recipe for baked walleye is one of his favorites.

- Dan Johnson, Senior Editor of the North American Fisherman, makes a delicious baked stuffed lake trout and you'll find out exactly how to prepare it, too.

If you're like me, you don't fish simply to put something on the table. But saving a few of the fish you do catch can lead to memorable meals, especially if you share them with good friends.

Take a few minutes to page through this great cookbook and imagine the possibilities. Word of warning, however. Don't do it on an empty stomach! Made that mistake, too!

Tight lines,

Steve

Steve Pennaz
Executive Director
North American Fishing Club

P.S. If you have a great recipe or two that you would like to share with your fellow NAFC members, please take a few minutes to jot down the ingredients needed, and the directions. Then mail it to us. Chances are, you'll see it in the 1997 edition of the NAFC Members' Cookbook!

Staff Members' Favorites

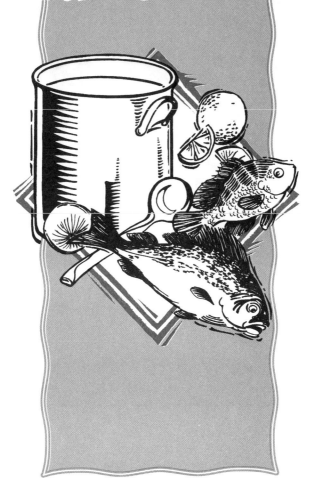

Steve Pennaz

Bachelor Special

½ lb. boneless fresh fish fillets per person
1 box corn flake crumbs
1 box fish batter mix
2 eggs
¾ cup milk
  vegetable or peanut oil

Empty box of corn flake crumbs into a 1 gallon resealable plastic bag. Add equal amounts of your favorite fish batter mix. Mix thoroughly. Beat eggs and milk, using enough to coat fillets (assume 1 egg for every 2 people). Heat ½" oil in large frying pan. Moisten fillets in egg, then coat with batter. Fry on both sides until golden brown.

Steve Pennaz
NAFC Staff

Jeff Boehler

Alice's Seviche

    1 lb. raw fish
      lemon or lime juice to cover fish
    2 large tomatoes, peeled and chopped
    1 large onion, chopped
    ¾ tsp. oregano
  2-3 jalapeno peppers, seeded and chopped
    2 T. olive oil
      salt and pepper to taste
      oregano to taste

Cut fish in bite-sized pieces, place in bowl and pour boiling water over to cover. Drain immediately. Sprinkle with lemon or lime juice and marinate about 2 hours.

Drain fish and combine with tomatoes, onions and peppers. Add enough olive oil to coat (don't make it too runny). Add salt, pepper and oregano to taste.

Serve with tostados or toasted tortillas.

Jeff Boehler
NAFC Staff

Dan Johnson

Baked Stuffed Lake Trout

1 lake trout
1 medium onion, chopped
3 stalks celery, chopped
3 cups fresh bread, cubed
½ lb. butter
salt and pepper

Gut and gill trout. Melt half the butter and saute celery and onion. Mix with bread, add more butter, and stuff fish with bread mixture. Brush remaining butter on skin of fish. Wrap trout in foil and bake at 350 degrees until thickest part of meat flakes easily.

Dan Johnson
NAFC Staff

Larry Sletten

Baked Parmesan Walleye

- 8 boneless walleye fillets
- 1 cup Italian bread crumbs, finely crushed
- 1 cup sour cream
- 2 tsp. onion salt
- 2 tsp. garlic salt
- 1 cup Parmesan cheese, grated

Preheat oven to 400 degrees. Lightly butter a 9" x 13" baking pan or dish. Wash and dry the fillets and arrange them evenly in the pan. Mix the remaining ingredients in a bowl and spread evenly over the walleye fillets. Bake 15-20 minutes until fish flakes easily with a fork. Place fish under broiler for a minute or two to lightly brown the top. Serve with fresh salad and your favorite pasta.

Larry Sletten
NAFC Staff

Kurt Beckstrom

Baked Pike

1-2 lbs. pike fillets
⅔ cup butter
⅔ cup crushed cracker crumbs
    salt, pepper, thyme, to taste
    lemon juice

If fillets are large, cut to portion size. Sprinkle with salt, pepper and thyme. Brown butter in shallow baking dish, and dip fillets in butter. Roll fillets in cracker crumbs and sprinkle with lemon juice to taste. Bake at 450 degrees until flesh flakes with fork (about 10 minutes for each inch of thickness).

Kurt Beckstrom
NAFC Staff

Barbecued "Snake"

When you've got a big northern on your stringer, and you don't have the time, talent or energy to fillet the thing, gut it, remove fins and cut cross-section into 1½" steaks (just like you might cut a salmon). Fire up the grill. Medium to low heat is best.

1 **Northern pike, cleaned**
½ **stick butter or margarine**
1 **T. chili sauce**
1 **tsp. Worcestershire sauce**
1 **tsp. Dijon mustard**
2 **tsp. lemon juice**

2 **dashes of Tabasco sauce**
½ **tsp. ground black pepper**
3 **shakes onion salt**
3 **shakes lemon pepper**

In a small saucepan, combine all ingredients. Heat until bubbling, stirring frequently. Baste fish steaks generously before putting on grill. Baste frequently while grilling. The more sauce you can get to drip down on the coals, the better.

On my grill, it takes about 4 minutes on each side to reach "perfect fish flakiness." Just be sure the meat has turned opaque white all the way through before serving. This stuff will stick like crazy if your grill isn't well seasoned. For best results, use a seafood cooker tray on your grill or use some thick aluminum foil under the fish. Makes a great

Forrest Fox

change of pace when you've had 6 deep-fried shore lunches in a row. Serves 1-20, depending on the size of the "snake." Great on salmon and trout, too.

Forrest Fox
NAFC Staff

17

Boundary Waters Baked Fish

1 man-made oven
1 cast iron skillet with
    long handle
2 boxes long grain and wild
    rice mix
    seasonings, such as Cajun
      spices, lemon pepper, etc.
    oil
    fish
    garlic cloves

Jay McNaughton

Build a camp oven. Put small amount of oil in pan, just enough to coat bottom. Chop and crush 1 garlic clove and spread around skillet. Pour rice and seasonings into skillet. Add enough water so rice begins to float freely. Season rice to taste. Press fish fillets into rice and water mixture and spread some rice and seasoning over fish. Cover skillet with aluminum foil or lid and place in oven. Cook until fish is flaky. Add more water as needed. Rice should be ready at the same time.

Next to the oven, on one side, set up an open fire pit. Grill or fry addition fish to go with the baked. On the other side, set up another open pit to boil water for coffee, cook linguini, etc.

Every year we also bake pizzas and German chocolate brownies in our oven. Our lake is about 12 hours of hard paddling with 5 portages into the Quetico Park located along the Minnesota and Canadian border. The longest portages are 1½ miles and ¾ miles, respectively. We eat better in the middle of nowhere than we do at home.

Jay McNaughton
NAFC Staff

Crappie with Garlic and Fresh Tomatoes

1½ lbs. boneless crappie, cut into 1-inch cubes
1 cup olive oil
⅓ cup green onions, chopped
1 tsp. fresh garlic, chopped
1 cup fresh tomatoes, diced
2 T. red wine vinegar
4 T. fresh parsley, chopped
salt and pepper to taste

Combine 2 tablespoons oil in saucepan with onions, garlic, tomatoes, vinegar, salt and pepper. In a frying pan, heat the remaining oil over high heat. Meanwhile season the crappie with salt and pepper. Fry the crappie cubes for one minute.

Immediately spoon the crappie cubes into the tomato mixture and cook over medium-high heat until the crappie pieces are done—about 4 minutes. Spoon onto serving plate and sprinkle with parsley.

Serve with rice or pasta and fresh vegetables.

Andrea Gohman
NAFC Staff

Andrea Gohman

19

Steve Pennaz

Fish in Lemon Butter Microwave

  1 lb. fish, boneless, chunked (walleye, crappie, bass, etc.)
¼ cup butter
  1 T. Worcestershire sauce
¼ cup chives
  3 tsp. lemon juice
½ tsp. salt
¼ tsp. Cayenne pepper
½ tsp. garlic powder

Put fish in glass baking dish and microwave on high for 1 minute. Combine rest of ingredients and spoon mixture over fish. Cover dish with waxed paper and microwave on high for 5-6 minutes or until fish flakes easily.

Steve Pennaz
NAFC Staff

Steve Pennaz

Fish Patties

4-5 lbs. diced, boneless fish (walleye, bass, pike, crappies, etc.)
 2 eggs, beaten
 1 cup shore lunch batter (or homemade version with flour, spices)
 ½ medium onion, chopped fine
 ¼ medium green pepper, diced egg plant, or zucchini (optional)
 ¾ cup milk

Combine all ingredients except eggs in large bowl. Add beaten eggs. Mixture should be firm but moist. Add flour as needed to thicken or milk to thin.

Heat frying pan to 325 degrees. Form mixture into patties and fry on each side until golden brown.

Steve Pennaz
NAFC Staff

Hush Puppies

  1 cup self-rising cornmeal
  1 cup self-rising flour
  ½ cup finely chopped onions
  2 eggs
    enough whole milk to make thick mixture

Mix all ingredients well (Batter should be thick but not dry). Drop teaspoons of mixture into hot fat or oil in deep fryer. Cook until brown. Serve hot.

Beth Metzen
NAFC Staff

French Lake Trout

1-2 lbs. lake trout steaks
  1 bottle French salad
    dressing

Cut trout into 1" steaks. Trim the belly meat and fat along the lateral lines. Place steaks in shallow baking dish and cover with bottled salad dressing. Cover with plastic wrap and refrigerate for 2-4 hours.

Drain steaks and oven broil or cook on a grill until the flesh flakes with a fork. Cooking time will depend on the size of the steaks.

Kurt Beckstrom

Delicious with fresh-baked cornbread and crisp garden salad. This recipe also works well with salmon and other trout species.

Kurt Beckstrom
NAFC Staff

Dan Kennedy

Lemon Pepper Grilled Fillets

4-6 good sized fillets (can use for any fish)
  1 bottle Lawry's Lemon Pepper Marinade
    lemon pepper
  1 onion, sliced

Cover fillets in marinade and refrigerate for 2-4 hours. Drain and lay fillets on double sheet of aluminum foil, greased. Fold edges and pour ½ cup marinade over fillets. Sprinkle with lemon-pepper. Add sliced onion and cover with foil. Grill over medium-high heat for 10-12 minutes or until fish flakes.

Dan Kennedy
NAFC Staff

Not So Lo-Cal Walleye Tempters

2 lbs. fresh walleye fillets
1-2 sleeves Ritz crackers
½ cup corn starch
3 eggs (depending on number of fillets)
   salt and pepper to taste
2 sticks butter or margarine

Rinse fillets thoroughly under cold water. Cut into small to medium-sized pieces. Place fillets in a bowl of cold water and chill for at least one hour.

Put crackers in a large resealable plastic bag. Close bag, releasing as much trapped air as possible. Using a rolling pin, crush the crackers to consistency you prefer. Pour onto a flat container.

Put corn starch in separate bowl.

In a medium-sized bowl, beat eggs well. Add salt and pepper to taste and mix well. Lay out double layer of paper towels on counter or plate. Prepare a serving plate with two layers of paper towels.

Rich Sundberg

When ready to begin cooking, melt one or two sticks of butter or margarine in large fry pan or electric skillet over medium heat.

Drain water from fillets and pat dry with paper towels. Roll fillets individually in the following order: corn starch, egg, crushed crackers. Place in frying pan and cook each side until golden brown.. Remove cooked fillets from skillet and place on serving plate with paper towels to remove excess butter. Serve immediately with fresh lemon, tartar sauce, etc.

If you're cooking a large quantity of fish, place cooked fish on paper towels and put in oven on low heat until ready to serve.

Rich Sundberg
NAFC Staff

Poached Perch

2-3 lbs. perch fillets
¼ cup water
¼ cup lemon juice
2 T. melted butter
2 tsp. salt
1 tsp. black pepper
1 tsp. thyme
1 small onion, finely chopped
1½ tsp. chopped parsley

Place fillets in an aluminum foil pouch. Sprinkle with salt and pepper. Pour lemon juice over them, followed by melted butter. Sprinkle with thyme, onion and parsley. Seal pouch and place on bed of coals for 20 minutes. Turn once. This recipe also works well with walleyes, northern pike and trout.

Kurt Beckstrom
NAFC Staff

Salmon Loaf

1 lb. cooked salmon, chopped
3 slices whole-grain bread cut in
    small cubes
1 tsp. salt
¼ cup butter, melted
½ cup onion, finely chopped
1 tsp. Dijon mustard
1 T. cooking sherry
1½ cups whole milk
2 eggs
parsley flakes
garlic cloves, chopped

Beat eggs in small bowl. Add bread, salt and butter. Heat milk, mustard and sherry to lukewarm and add to first mixture. Add salmon. Mix thoroughly, place in greased loaf pan. Bake in preheated 350-degree oven for 1 hour. Garnish with parsley flakes and freshly chopped garlic cloves.

Beth Metzen
NAFC Staff

Salmon Stew

- 1 cup cooked salmon
- 3 cups whole milk
- ¼ cup cream
- 1 T. butter
- ½ cup tomatoes, finely chopped and cooked
- 2 tsp. sugar
  salt and pepper to taste
  shredded cheddar cheese for garnish

Heat milk, cream and butter to scalding. Add tomatoes, sugar and salmon. Remove from heat. Add salt and pepper to taste. Cover tightly for five minutes. Stir and garnish with shredded cheddar cheese. Serve hot.

Beth Metzen
NAFC Staff

Simply Delicious Walleye

So simple—but so delicious. You'll think you're at the finest of restaurants.

- 1 lb. walleye fillets
- 6 T. butter
- 3 oz. slivered almonds
- 1 T. lemon juice
- 1 T. chopped parsley
  salt and pepper to taste

Melt butter in large skillet. Stir in almonds until golden brown. Add walleye and sear on one side. Turn fillets and cook on medium until just done. Meat should be white all the way through (pry fish apart with fork for inspection). Squirt fish with lemon juice and top with parsley. Spoon almonds over fillets.

Steve Pennaz
NAFC Staff

Spruce Center Creek Trout

6 trout, around 10 inches each
¼ cup flour
1 stick butter
¼ cup almond slivers

If you clean your trout streamside, which is best, pick up all entrails, put them in a plastic bag and take them home to your garbage pail.

Clean fish well, including scaling them. Dust lightly in flour and fry in ⅔ stick butter. Do not overcook. Remove from frying pan and bone carefully (in same manner as for bluegill). Place two fillets of each fish on a hotplate. Simmer the almond slivers in ⅓ stick butter for 5 minutes. Spoon over trout and serve. Usually serves 6 adults.

Jeff Boehler
NAFC Staff

Tangy Fish Delight

fish fillets
1 clove garlic
olive oil to cover bottom of pan
1 small can tomato paste
1 cup orange juice
pasta

In large skillet over medium heat, brown garlic in olive oil. Add tomato paste and orange juice to desired consistency. Add fish fillets. Cover and simmer slowly until fish is done, about 5-10 minutes, depending on thickness of fillets. Serve over pasta.

Kelly Gohman
NAFC Staff

Kelly Gohman

27

Walleye in Butter

2 lbs. walleye fillets
¼ cup butter
1 T. Worcestershire sauce
¼ cup green onions, chopped
2 tsp. lemon juice
½ tsp. salt
1 clove garlic, minced
¼ tsp. cayenne pepper

Combine all ingredients except fish in saucepan and heat to boiling. Wash and dry fillets; place in baking pan. Pour butter mixture over fish and bake at 375 degrees for 35-45 minutes.

Recipe is from my friend Bob Schranck's long list of tasty dishes and his book *Wild in the Kitchen*.

Dan Johnson
NAFC Staff

Dan Johnson

Salmon Marinade

½ cup soy sauce
1 T. sugar
2 tsp. lemon juice
½ tsp. ginger
1 clove garlic, minced
2 T. dry sherry or dry white wine

Marinate salmon, skin side up, one and a half hours. Grill skin side down for 15 minutes.

Michele Bursey
NAFC Staff

Kevin's Poached Pike in Lemon Sauce

4 lb. pike
salt
whole peppercorns
1 medium onion
parsley
2 egg yolks
1 tsp. sugar

Skin and bone pike, then cover fish with water. Add salt, pepper, onion, parsley, and a tablespoon of lemon juice. Poach and reserve 1 cup of stock in pot.

Sauce

Beat eggs yolks, add lemon rind and remaining juice. Pour very slowly into hot stock, stirring constantly and cook until thick. To further thicken add another beaten egg yolk. Add the sugar and parsley and serve with fish.

Kevin Hagen
NAFC Staff

Kevin Hagen

Fish Fillets Almondine

fish fillets, walleye or northern pike
2 T. butter or margarine
　　per fillet
1 tsp. lemon juice per fillet
　　paprika
　　lemon pepper
　　bread crumbs, very fine
　　almond slices

Arrange fillets in baking dish, melt butter and add lemon juice to the butter. Pour over fillets covering them completely with the lemon butter mixture. Sprinkle with paprika, lemon pepper and bread crumbs. Bake at 450 degrees for 8-15 minutes or until fish flakes easily. Add almonds in the last 2 minutes of baking and watch carefully.

Mary Mackie
NAFC Staff

Mary Mackie

NAFC Members' Favorites

Bass Au Gratin

1 lb. bass fillets
2 T. cracker crumbs
1 cup canned tomatoes
2 T. onion, chopped
¼ tsp. salt
⅛ tsp. pepper
1 T. butter
¼ cup cheddar cheese, grated

Sprinkle cracker crumbs in greased 1-qt. shallow baking dish. Place fillets on crumbs. Combine tomatoes, onion, salt and pepper. Pour over fillets. Dot with butter, sprinkle with cheese. Bake at 350 degrees for 35 minutes or until fish flakes easily with fork. This recipe works with perch fillets as well.

Charles Kirby
Sweet Springs, Missouri

Baked Bass

2 lbs. fish bass
½ cup butter
   salt, pepper, paprika to taste
2 T. lemon juice
1 cup white wine
2 cups cheddar cheese, grated
½ cup Parmesan cheese, grated

Brown butter in baking dish. Sprinkle fish with salt and pepper to taste and place in butter. Sprinkle with lemon juice and paprika. Pour wine over fish. Bake 10 minutes at 350 degrees or until fish flakes. Baste, cover with cheese, and broil. Serve with pasta and salad.

Steven Owens
Flagstaff, Arizona

Bass Burritos

1 lb. bass fillets, chopped
½ stick butter
1 large onion, chopped coarsely
1 red pepper, chopped
1 green pepper, chopped
  garlic salt, onion salt, lemon pepper, to taste
8 flour tortillas, large
  hot sauce or salsa
3 lemons or limes, quartered

Fry chunks of fillets in butter with onions, peppers, and seasonings until done. Warm tortillas. Spoon into tortillas, and garnish with hot sauce, salsa and lemon or lime wedges.

Brett L. Southern
San Diego, California

Bass in Wine Sauce

2 lbs. bass fillets, cut into
  serving pieces
  salt and pepper
  flour
6 T. olive oil

2 shallots, finely chopped
2 anchovy fillets, chopped
1 tsp. parsley flakes
1 cup dry white wine
¼ cup chicken stock

Season bass with salt and pepper. Roll lightly in flour. Heat 4 tablespoons olive oil in a skillet. Cook fish over moderate heat until brown on both sides.

In a saucepan, heat 2 tablespoons olive oil. Add shallots, anchovies and parsley flakes. Simmer slowly until shallots soften. Add wine and simmer until wine is reduced by one-fourth. Add stock, salt and pepper to taste and simmer another 3-4 minutes. Pour sauce over fish and simmer 1-2 minutes to blend all flavors.

Bryan Lasher
Union City, Pennsylvania

Mike Ciechowski

Grilled Bass Fillets

2 lbs. bass fillets	¼ tsp. salt
1 lemon, halved	⅛ tsp. oregano, crushed
1 T. celery, finely chopped	⅛ tsp. freshly ground pepper
2 T. onion, finely chopped	⅓ cup sliced almonds
2 T. parsley flakes	1 T. butter, melted

Rub fillets with juice from half of lemon. In small bowl, combine celery, onion, parsley, salt, oregano and pepper. Mix well. Sprinkle mixture on both sides of fillets. Combine nuts and butter.

Important: Remove cooking grids from grill. Preheat grill on high 5 minutes, then turn controls down to medium-low. Return grids to grill and brush with oil. This prevent the fish from sticking to hot metal.

Squeeze remaining lemon half over fillets; arrange fish on grill. Cover grill and cook 10-12 minutes or until fish flakes easily with fork. During last 5 minutes, sprinkle nuts over fish.

Mike Ciechowski
South Windsor, Connecticut

Carolina Hash

4 good-sized bass, perch or stripers (about 3 lbs.)
2 medium onions, diced
1 lb. sliced bacon, cut into small squares
6 large white potatoes, diced and boiled

Bring a large pot of water to a boil. Add potatoes and cook until fork tender, about 10 minutes

Scale and clean fish, removing all bones except spine. Boil fish until done (about 10 minutes).

Fry bacon in skillet until golden brown. Pour bacon and grease into small bowl.

While bacon, potatoes and fish are steaming hot, place each item on table separately. Each diner then puts a good amount of potatoes, fish, onions on plate. After picking remaining bones from fish, mix ingredients into hash. Then spoon bacon bits and grease over hash. You now have the best fish dinner a poor boy could wish for. Salt and pepper to taste.

R. D. (Dan) Hall
Wharton, Texas

Dilly Bass

4 bass fillets
1 stick butter
¼ tsp. dill seeds
1 tsp. bottled lemon juice
½ tsp. garlic powder
　Ritz cracker crumbs
½ cup Parmesan cheese, grated

Melt butter and add dill seeds, lemon juice and garlic powder. Mix well. Dip fish into butter mixture, then dredge in cracker crumbs and place in glass baking dish. Sprinkle generously with grated Parmesan cheese. Bake at 350 degrees for about 15 minutes or until done.

Gordon Alpha
Lake Charles, California

Easy Fried Bass

2 lbs. bass fillets or whole
   salt and pepper
½ cup prepared Italian, Caesar, or Russian salad dressing
1 cup dry bread or cracker crumbs.

Sprinkle fish with salt and pepper. Dip into salad dressing, then into crumbs. Fry in small amount of hot oil in frying pan until crisp and fish flakes. Serve with lemon.

Ronnie Story
Jones, Oklahoma

Bass with Lemon and Butter

2-3 lbs. bass fillets (or other firm fish, such as snook, yellow tail, etc.)
 ½ cup all-purpose flour
 2 T. butter
 1 lemon, quartered
   salt and pepper to taste

Place fillets on flat surface and season both sides with salt and pepper to taste. Let sit for 10 minutes. Dust fillets with flour, shaking off excess. Melt butter in skillet on medium-high heat. When butter starts to bubble, place fillets in skillet. Turn several times until golden brown. Then sprinkle lemon juice liberally over both sides. Serve with baked beans and coleslaw

Robert Creighton
Naples, Florida

Jimmy, Maria and Ciora's Striped Bass Fry

1 whole striped bass, filleted or cut into steaks
2 cups flour
1 cup cornstarch
1 egg, beaten
1 T. mayonnaise

Combine flour, cornstarch, egg and mayonnaise in bowl. Dip bass in mixture and fry until browned.

Jimmy Romero
Rockaway Park, New York

John's Favorite Bass

2 lbs. bass fillets
  salt and pepper
1 pkg. Shake and Bake for Pork (Original Recipe)
3 T. flour
  milk
  oil to cover bottom of skillet

Lay fish on a plate and salt and pepper them lightly on both sides. Cover with waxed paper and put in refrigerator for about 2 hours. Add flour to crumbs and mix well. Moisten fish in a little milk, then dip in crumb mixture. Fry in cooking oil, preferably in electric skillet heated to 350 degrees. Brown on both sides. You can also deep fry using instructions on package. If you prefer baked fish, after coating fillets with crumbs, lay them on well-greased pan and bake 15-20 minutes at 350 degrees.

John Kraemer
Milwaukee, Wisconsin

Oven-Baked Bass

4 medium-sized bass, whole
2 large onions, sliced
1 lemon, sliced
¼ cup butter, melted
¼ tsp. garlic powder
  salt and pepper

Place bass in baking pan. Combine onions, lemon, butter and garlic powder in a large bowl. Toss until onions are well-coated with other ingredients. Pour over bass. Salt and pepper to taste. Cover with aluminum foil. Bake at 400 degrees until tender.

Robert Bower
Charlotte, North Carolina

McWilliams' McFish Fillets

8 fish fillets, your choice
1 cup water or beer
1 cup flour
1 egg
4 tsp. cornstarch
1 tsp. salt
1 tsp. baking powder
¼ cup salad oil
¼ tsp. garlic powder

Mix all ingredients except fish to make batter. Dip fillets in batter and deep fry at 375 degrees until as golden as a sunset on a Missouri pond.

Brandon McWilliams

Brandon McWilliams
Wichita, Kansas

Pan Broiled Black Bass

4 boneless bass fillets, medium-sized
3 T. butter or margarine
2 T. lemon juice
2 T. garlic salt
  Cajun Creole seasoning

Over medium heat in large skillet, melt butter or margarine and add lemon juice. Put fillets in pan and sprinkle with garlic salt and Cajun seasonings. Cook until tender.

Mark Hafer
Dawsonville, Georgia

Rainy-Day Chowder

1 largemouth bass, filleted
1-2 cups milk
1 can of your favorite cream soup
1 large potato, cubed
½ cup peas, fresh or frozen
½ cup corn, frozen or canned
½ cup fresh or frozen carrots, sliced
½ can mushrooms
  salt and freshly ground pepper
  garlic and thyme (optional)

In large saute pan, poach bass in milk until the meat flakes (fish should be covered in milk while cooking). Add other ingredients, including spices to taste. Simmer over low heat until vegetables are cooked. Serve with freshly baked dinner biscuits and white wine.

Shelley Rizzo
Sault Ste. Marie, Ontario

Succulent Simplicity:
Bacon-Baked Bass

3-6 lbs. bass, whole
  seasoned salt or lemon pepper
1 large onion, sliced, rings separated
  bacon strips
¼ cup milk
  lemon slices

Lay cleaned fish on greased heavy-duty aluminum foil in baking pan. Slice through exposed skin vertically at 2" intervals. Season exposed side liberally with seasoned salt or lemon pepper. Lay onion rings across fish, followed by bacon strips on top of onion.

Fold up sides of foil; add milk and secure carefully. Bake at 350 degrees for 30-40 minutes, depending on size of fish. Open top of foil to expose bacon; then broil until bacon browns. Remove from oven and serve immediately. Have plenty of sliced lemon available and maybe a side dish of seviche. For a special treat, include oysters and shrimp with baked fish.

Norm Carpenter
San Antonio, Texas

Bass Baked with Vegetables

1½-2 lbs. fish fillets or inch-thick steaks
¼ lb. salt pork, cut into small cubes
1 onion, diced
¾ cup fresh mushrooms
¼ cup red or green pepper, diced
2 medium carrots, sliced thin
½ cup celery, sliced
1 tsp. dill weed
2 T. fresh chopped parsley
1 lemon, sliced
⅛ tsp. pepper
1 cup dry Sherry or white wine

In a skillet, fry the salt pork until crisp and golden. Add the onion, mushrooms, green pepper, carrots, celery, dill weed and parsley. Cook until tender.

In a buttered baking dish, add the cooked vegetables, and place fish on top.

Add the lemon slices and pour the wine over them. Cover with foil and bake in a 400 degree oven for about 10 minutes. Remove the foil, baste fish and continue to cook about 10 minutes or until the fish flakes when tested with a fork and has browned a bit.

Serve with mashed potatoes or rice, a brown and serve loaf of French bread and a green salad.

Lou Bignami
Moscow, Idaho

Bass Louie

The best bass for this is striped bass as the dish is a variation of the famous San Francisco Fisherman's Wharf Crab Louie. Striped bass, if steamed or poached is so close to crab body meat that restaurants used to substitute it for more expensive crab. These days it's illegal to sell striped bass caught in California. Black bass and, in particular, smallmouth from colder waters work, too. So does walleye and a number of other white meat fish like halibut. The last, if poached in water with a little sugar added, turns out very like lobster.

1½ lbs. cooked bass, flaked
 1 head lettuce, cored and shredded
 2 hard cooked eggs, sliced
 2 medium fresh tomatoes, sliced
16 cooked asparagus spears, cooled

Louie Dressing
 1 cup mayonnaise
 ¼ cup catsup, seasoned if you like
 3 T. lemon juice
   Dash hot sauce

Arrange lettuce on dishes. Mound on fish and decorate with sliced eggs, tomato and asparagus.

Combine dressing ingredients and serve separately so guests can pour on just the right amount. A wonderful lunch with Sour Dough French bread and butter.

Lou Bignami
Moscow, Idaho

Bass Fritters with Salsa

You can make this recipe with commercial salsa/taco sauce. Try a chunky style salsa with it's "heat" adjusted to your taste if you do. However, fresh salsa is very easy and very inexpensive to make, and it works well here, in tacos or as a dip.

Change the fritters to half-dollar size fish balls, fish sticks or half dollar-size fritters and you've a wonderful hor d'oeuvre, too.

- 1 cup cooked bass, flaked
- ¼ cup fish stock or clam juice
- ¼ cup milk
- 1 egg
- 3 T. butter, melted
- ¾ cup seasoned bread crumbs
- 2 T. grated onion
- 1 T. parsley flakes
- ¼ cup cooking oil

Heat oil in a pan over medium heat (about 375 degrees in a electric skillet works nicely).

Combine remaining ingredients, form into ¼ inch thick patties and cook on both sides until brown. Remove to drain on paper towels and keep warm until needed.

Salsa:

- 1 T. oil
- 1 green pepper, diced
- 1 medium onion, dice
- 1 green chili pepper, finely chopped
- ½ tsp. ground coriander
- ½ tsp. ground cumin
- ¼ tsp. sugar
- salt and pepper to taste
- ½ lb. fresh diced, chopped

Heat oil in a pot and cook the onion and pepper until barely colored. Add the chopped chili, coriander and cook two or three minutes.

Add remaining ingredients and cook for about five minutes. Note: a small amount of tomato paste may be added for color.

Lou Bignami
Moscow, Idaho

Sweet & Sour Bass

A two pound bass feeds two, a four pound bass feeds four, and sweet and sour bass offers a unique centerpiece to a Chinese meal. Serve it with a vegetable and fried rice and you're in for a treat.

2½-4 lb. bass
  2 T. dry sherry
  5 dime-sized slices of fresh ginger
  ½ cup sugar
  6 T. rice or white wine vinegar
  1 T. dark soy sauce
  2 T. arrowroot
  2 cloves of garlic, crushed
  1 carrot, peeled and shredded as finely as possible
  1 small can bamboo shoots, shredded

Cut the fish three times on each side in line with the ribs.

Trim all fins except dorsal fin - the "doneness" indicator.

Boil enough water in a deep pan or wok to cover the fish.

Add the fish, sherry and ginger. Cover the pot and remove from the heat as fish cooks about 10 minutes per each inch of thickness, (it's done when the dorsal fin pulls out).

Remove fish from wok or pot and keep it warm as you boil the remaining ingredients until the sauce thickens. Pour some sauce over the fish and serve the rest in a small pitcher.

Lou Bignami
Moscow, Idaho

Bass with Black Butter

You need fillets for this wonderful, easy to make classic that also suits crappie and most panfish from cold, clear waters. Since you remove the skin after the fish cooks, it's a solid choice in waters that might yield a muddy or other dubious tastes. If you're near saltwater, try it with skate or ray wings, sand dabs, petrale or halibut.

6-8 bass fillets (enough to serve four)
  2 slices of onion
    salt
  6 black peppercorns
    water (enough to cover all ingredients)

Black Butter:

  4 T. butter
  2 T. white wine vinegar
  1 tsp. capers, drained
  1 tsp. chopped parsley for garnish

Put the fillets in a pan, add the next four ingredients, bring to a boil, reduce heat and poach until fish flakes, about ten minutes.

Carefully lift out the fillets onto a heated serving dish.

Cook the butter in a small pan over high heat until it starts to brown. Add capers and remove pan from heat. Add the vinegar so the butter bubbles. Pour over fish, sprinkle with parsley and serve immediately.

One theory suggests a drunk Cajun cook burned the redfish version of this dish, and, rather than toss the dish out, served it to a bunch of Yankees. When they asked what the dish was they were told, "Any fool can see it's blackened Redfish."

Lou Bignami
Moscow, Idaho

Herb Grilled Bluegill Fillets

The key to this recipe is fresh herbs — fresh dill, fresh tarragon and other favorite herbs also work. You can freeze water-covered green herbs in ice cube trays and stash the cubes in a bag until needed, too. Beats winter herb prices for the snow belt set.

¾ lb. bluegill fillets
⅓ cup olive oil
2 T. lemon juice
1 garlic clove, minced

3 T. fresh rosemary leaves
¼ tsp. Worcestershire sauce
½ tsp. pepper

Rinse fillets and pat dry. In a small bowl, mix oil, lemon juice, garlic, rosemary, Worcestershire sauce and pepper.

Over charcoal-gray coals, grill fish while basting with marinade until brown, about 5 minutes a side or until fish flakes with a fork.

Lou Bignami
Moscow, Idaho

Panfish Bluegill Stroganofff

1½ lbs. bluegill fillets, not over
　　½ inch thick
1 T. butter or margarine
1 cup plain yogurt
1 garlic clove, minced
2 green onions, chopped

½ cup mushrooms, sliced
½ tsp. paprika
1 tsp. dry dillweed
　salt and pepper
1 lemon, thinly sliced

Rinse fillets and pat dry. Arrange in a single layer in a buttered baking dish. Top with mushrooms.

Salt and pepper to taste.

In a small bowl combine yogurt, garlic, onions, paprika and dillweed. Spread mixture over each fillet and top each fillet with a lemon slice. Bake 30 minutes in 350 degree oven.

Lou Bignami
Moscow, Idaho

Bluegill Oriental

Even "one bite" sized bluegill fillets offer a delicious taste treat with this fine Japanese recipe that also works for small perch, sunfish or crappie fillets. Add some sliced zucchini, carrots or onion. You can also coat with flour and deep fry and serve on rice for a lovely meal that requires little preparation time.

     2 lbs. panfish fillets
    ½ cup flour
    ½ cup cornstarch
     1 tsp. salt
    1½ tsp. baking powder
     1 egg
    ⅔ cup water
       cooking oil
       catsup
       Chinese hot mustard

Rinse and cut fillets into bitesized pieces. Combine flour, cornstarch, salt and baking powder. Beat egg and water together and mix quickly with dry ingredients. Batter should be a little lumpy.

Heat one-inch of oil in a skillet over medium heat. Dip fillets into batter and fry quickly on each side until brown, about 2-3 minutes. Drain on a paper towel.

Serve with catsup, mustard and/or a little soy sauce for dip. Note: this batter also works well as a coating for vegetable tempura made from sliced squash, carrots or zucchini.

Lou Bignami
Moscow, Idaho

Broiled Marinated Carp

3-4 lbs. carp, dressed and split
⅓ cup oil
½ cup thin onion rings
2 T. lemon juice
1½ tsp. salt
½ tsp. pepper
1½ tsp. basil, crushed

Rinse carp with cold water and pat dry with paper towels. To make marinade, combine oil, onions, lemon juice, salt, pepper, basil and 3 tablespoons water in a jar. Cover tightly and shake until well blended.

Put the carp in a shallow baking dish. Cover with marinade, and let stand at room temperature for 1 hour.

Preheat the broiler. Place fish, skin side down, on a well-buttered piece of foil on the broiler pan. Spoon on the marinade. Place pan 4" under broiler and cook 10 minutes until the meat is opaque throughout.

Cheryl Birch
Lublin, Wisconsin

Fish Fritters

During gigging season, we can our own carp and suckers. This is what we use in this recipe, but any canned fish would work.

1 lb. canned fish, chunked
1 egg, beaten
½ cup flour
dash of pepper
2 tsp. baking powder

Mix all ingredients well to make a thick batter. Drop by teaspoonfuls into hot oil and fry until golden brown. Eat while hot.

Leonard Mincks
Halfway, Missouri

Carp a la Smashé

I know a lot of people turn up their noses at the lowly carp. But I guarantee if you use this recipe you'll be very happy. Pay close attention to the liquid amounts.

1 clean soft-wood plank, 2 inches longer than carp

Clean and scale carp and place on plank in baking pan. Add the following:

4 oz. bourbon
4 oz. gin
4 oz. scotch
4 oz. vodka

Cover and bake in 150-degree oven for 15 minutes. Remove and add:

6 oz. amaretto
6 oz. cream de menthe
6 oz. coffee liqueur
6 oz. apple brandy

Cover and return to oven. Bake 1 more hour. Remove from oven and set carp and plank aside. Pour remaining liquid in a large glass to cool. Add ice if necessary. Wait 20 minutes for everything to cool.

Throw carp in garbage. Drink all liquid. Then eat the plank. This is the best way, by far, that I've found to dine on carp.

Dan Olsen
Graeagle, California

Dave's Pickled Fish

1 lb. carp fillets, sliced
1 large onion, sliced
    canning salt, as needed
    white vinegar, as needed

In a plastic bucket or stone crock, use canning salt to make a brine strong enough to float an egg. Soak fish in brine for 48 hours, covered with a plate. Drain but do not rinse. Cover well with white vinegar and stir daily for at least 4-5 days. Drain off vinegar but do not rinse fish.

Make pickling solution as follows:
    2 cups white vinegar
    1 cup sugar
    1 cup white wine
    1 T. pickling spices

Boil solution 5 minutes, then cool completely. Layer fish and sliced onions in large-mouth jars. Cover with cool pickling solution, leaving ½" headspace.

Refrigerate for 7 days, turning jars each day. Be sure canning lids are secure. I boil the lids before I put them on so the rubber seal is soft. I also use lots of onions. I like them pickled, too.

Dave DeBolt
Des Moines, Iowa

Anna's Favorite Fish Nuggets

    4 fish fillets
    5 T. Dijon mustard
    ½ tsp. garlic powder
    ¼ tsp. cayenne pepper
    ½ tsp. Onion powder
       salt
       yellow cornmeal

Pat fillets with paper towels to remove excess moisture and cut into bite-sized pieces.

In bowl, mix mustard and seasonings. Add fish nuggets and stir, covering each piece well. Roll in corn meal to coat. Fry in hot oil until golden brown.

Clayton Schmidt
Commerce Township, Michigan

California Fried Fish

    1 lb. fish fillets
    2 eggs, beaten
    ½ cup fine cornmeal
    ½ cup flour
    ½ cup Parmesan cheese
       Italian herbs
       seasoned salt
       lemon pepper
    3 T. olive oil
    3 T. butter

Measure cornmeal, flour, and Parmesan cheese into a 1 gallon resealable plastic bag. Add dash of Italian herbs, along with seasoned salt and lemon pepper to bag. Dip fillets in beaten egg, place fish in bag, and shake well to cover. Fry in olive oil and butter.

Dan Jones
Petaluma, California

Country Panfried Fish

2 lb. fish fillets
1 tsp. salt
¼ tsp. pepper
1 egg
1 T. water
1 cup cornmeal
   shortening or vegetable oil

Sprinkle both sides of fillets with salt and pepper. Beat egg and water until thoroughly blended. Dip fillets in egg and water mixture, then coat with cornmeal. Put shortening or oil in frying pan (about ⅛"-¼" oil, depending on thickness of fish) and heat until hot. Fry fish over medium heat, turning carefully, until golden brown on both sides.

Samuel Gontkovsky
Davie, Florida

English Fish and Chips

1 lb. fish fillets
2 eggs, separated
1 cup flour
½ cup beer
¼ cup milk
½ tsp. salt
¼ tsp. black pepper

Beat egg yokes until thick and light. Blend in beer, milk, flour and seasonings until smooth.

Beat egg whites until stiff but not dry. Fold egg whites into batter. Dip fish fillets in batter and deep fry at 375 degrees 2-3 minutes or until golden brown and puffy. Drain fish on paper towel. French fry potatoes to serve with fish. The English serve this with malt vinegar.

Ralph Finizio
Auburn, New York

Fried Lemony Fish

1 lb. fish fillets
2 cups plain cornmeal
3 T. self-rising flour
1 tsp. salt

1 tsp. black pepper
½ tsp. cayenne pepper
2 heaping T. lemon herb seasoning
cooking oil for deep frying

Mix all dry ingredients well. Drain fish and lay on folded towel. Cover with another towel and gently mash out most of the water.

Cut fish into small pieces 1" x 2". Crappie fillets can be cut in half. Put fish in dry mix and stir until completely covered. Deep fry until golden brown. Drain on paper towels.

Robert N. Cassetty
Hendersonville, Tennessee

Fried Fish New Orleans

2 lb. fish fillets, cut into 1½ inch squares
Tabasco sauce to taste
2 eggs, beaten
¾ cup water
¾ cup flour
¼ cup cornstarch
¼ tsp. baking powder
salt and black pepper, freshly ground, to taste
peanut oil for deep frying

Place fish and Tabasco sauce in a stainless steel bowl. Let marinate for 20 minutes. Start the batter by whipping the eggs and adding the water. Then blend the flour, cornstarch, baking powder, salt and pepper together in a dry bowl, using a fork. Gently stir this into the egg/water mixture. Do not try to get out all the small lumps. It will not matter. Do not overmix.

Heat 4 cups peanut oil to 375-400 degrees. Dip the marinated fish squares in the batter and deep fry until light brown (about 4 minutes).

Dale Jenkins
Fairfield Bay, Arkansas

Golden Fried Fish

1 lb. fish fillets
⅔ cup corn starch
⅔ cup cornmeal
⅓ cup flour
4 tsp. baking powder
2 tsp. salt
1 tsp. oil
1 egg

Combine all ingredients except fish. Add enough water to make batter about the consistency of heavy whipping cream.

Roll fish fillets in flour, then dip them in the batter. Allow excess to drip off. Deep fry in skillet of hot oil, until golden brown or fish floats. You may need to turn fish a couple of times while cooking. Remove fish and allow them to drain a few minutes before serving.

Kirk Baird
Bradleyville, Missouri

Pan-Fried Fillets of Fish

1 lb. fish fillets
1 T. mayonnaise
1 T. milk
½ tsp. salt
¼ tsp. pepper
1 cup fine cracker crumbs
fat or oil

Blend mayonnaise, milk, salt and pepper. Dip fillets in mayonnaise mixture, then in cracker crumbs, coating all sides well.

Heat fat in heavy skillet. Add fish and fry over moderate heat until golden brown on both sides.

Serve with lemon wedges, tartar sauce, mayonnaise or salsa.

Jerry Solberg
Weyauwega, Wisconsin

Tom's Pan-Fried Fish

½ lb. fish fillets
1 cup sour cream
1 cup bread crumbs, your choice

Soak fish in sour cream overnight. Roll in bread crumbs and fry in a hot frying pan with very little oil until fish is fork tender.

Tom Bennett
North Pole, Arkansas

Charcoal-Grilled Fish

1 fish, whole
butter
lemon juice
Tabasco sauce
dry Italian salad dressing mix

Use butter, lemon juice and a dash of Tabasco to make a basting sauce.

Fillet fish, leaving skin and scales intact.

Rub fish on all sides with dry Italian salad dressing mix and refrigerate about 2 hours.

Cook (scales down) over a medium charcoal fire, covered. Baste occasionally being careful not to overcook. Fish is done when it first starts to flake. Do not turn. Serve hot, scooping fish away from skin and scales.

Rene Broussard
New Iberia, Louisiana

Fish on the Grill

1 lb. fish fillets
lemon pepper seasoning
garlic powder
Mrs. Dash
½ onion, chopped
½ stick butter or margarine

Spread out a sheet of aluminum foil large enough to hold fillets. Cut fish into 3"
pieces and place on foil. Sprinkle fish with lemon pepper and garlic powder. Add
chopped onions as desired.

Slice butter or margarine and place on fish. Fold foil edges over, keeping fish flat.
Double wrap to prevent butter from dripping out.

Place foil pack over medium heat on grill and cook for about 20 minutes. Cooking
time and temperature may vary by grill.

Roxann Hopfauf
Mandan, North Dakota

Fish with Apricot Sauce

1 large fish, whole
apricot preserves
lemon pepper

Remove meat from bone, leaving skin and scales on. Spread well with apricot
preserves and lemon pepper. Grill, skin side down, over low heat. Cook as long as
you can stand to wait.

Dan (Jack) Auld, Jr.
Hunt, Texas

Barbecue Chili Fish

    6 8-oz. fillets
    ½ cup barbecue sauce
    ¼ cup reduced-calorie mayonnaise
    3 cloves garlic, minced
    1 tsp. chili sauce

In medium bowl, combine barbecue sauce, mayonnaise, garlic and chili sauce. Brush over fish fillets. Refrigerate, covered, at least 1 hour or overnight.

Place grill rack 5" from coals.

Set large skillet with flameproof handle on rack. Heat skillet and add fish. Cook, turning once, until fish flakes easily when tested with a fork.

Floyd T. Smith
Troy, North Carolina

Cajun Days Fresh Fillets

    4 fish fillets, 6 oz. each
    ⅓ cup flour
    ¼ tsp. black pepper
    ¼ tsp. Cajun spices
    2 egg whites
    1 tsp. paprika
    ¼ tsp. garlic salt
    1 T. canola oil

Blend flour, pepper, Cajun spices and paprika. Whisk egg whites and garlic salt together.

Heat oil in skillet at medium-high heat. Coat fillets with egg white lightly on both sides.

Dip in flour mixture and fry until fillets flake easily with a fork—about 5 minutes. Turn fillets over only once for best results.

Lisa J. Beach
Durham, North Carolina

Fish a la Creole

  2 lb. fresh fish, cut into 1-inch pieces
  2 T. olive oil
  2 cups green onions, trimmed
      and chopped
  ½ cup onions, chopped
  ½ cup parsley, chopped
  ½ cup green bell pepper, chopped
  ½ cup dry white wine
  1 T. garlic, chopped
  3 cups canned tomatoes chopped, with liquid
  1 cup vegetable or tomato juice
      cayenne pepper to taste
  1 T. Worcestershire sauce

Over medium-high heat in a large skillet, heat the olive oil and saute the green onion, onions, parsley and bell pepper until the onions are tender. Add the wine and garlic and continue cooking for 10 minutes. Stir in the tomatoes, vegetable juice, cayenne and Worcestershire sauce; stir to mix well.

Cover, reduce heat to medium and continue to cook for another 20 minutes or until the tomatoes fall apart. Add the fish, reduce the heat to low and simmer until the fish is done (about 20-30 minutes). Serve hot over cooked rice.

This is great with any whitefish, but it is outstanding when made with steelhead or salmon.

James D. Bates
Hermiston, Oregon

Fish Escabecki

1 lb. fish fillets	½ cup green olives, chopped
salt and pepper	¼ cup red cooking wine
1 cup flour	½ cup olive oil
1 onion, sliced	½ cup white vinegar

Clean and skin fish and cut into strips.

Season the fish with salt and pepper or your favorite seasoning. Flour fish on all sides and pan fry in hot oil in a skillet until lightly browned. Drain off excess oil and let cool for about 15 minutes.

Put 6-8 pieces of fish in a large bowl. Cover fish with onions and olives. Add vinegar, olive oil, and red wine. Let fish soak in this at least 2 hours, turning often. Garnish fish with parsley and slices of lemon. Serve with rice.

Fermin J. Bermejo
Shenandoah, Pennsylvania

Fish on a Stick

4 medium to large fish fillets	1 T. cider vinegar
1 T. orange rind, finely grated	1 T. sugar
½ cup orange juice	1-2 tsp. ground ginger
1 T. oil	1 tsp. sesame oil
2 T. soy sauce	wooden skewers soaked in water

In resealable plastic bag, combine orange rind, orange juice, oil, soy sauce, vinegar, sugar, ginger and sesame oil. Shake until well mixed. Place fillets in bag with marinade and refrigerate for 1 hour.

Remove fish, reserving marinade. Cut fillets lengthwise into strips about 1" wide. Thread fish on skewers to form an S shape. Place skewered fish fillets on preheated grill over high heat or oven-broil on greased rack.

Baste frequently with reserved marinade, turning once until fish is done (about 6-8 minutes, depending on thickness of fish). Serve hot over rice of your choice, such as fried or Cajun.

J. A. Jim Sutherland
Calgary, Alberta

Viskoekjes (Fish Cakes, Dutch Style)

These fish cakes can be made with any leftover fish, provided all bones are removed. Fish cakes are usually kept simple as far as flavor is concerned, but a little chopped onion can be added for extra flavor

½-1 lb. cooked fish
  4 slices white bread
    milk
  1 egg, lightly beaten
    salt and pepper
  2 T. chopped parsley
  1 egg, beaten
    toasted bread crumbs
1½ oz. butter or margarine
  1 lemon

Break boneless fish into small pieces. Remove the crusts from the bread, soak bread in milk, squeeze dry and mix with fish. Add the lightly beaten egg, salt and pepper to taste and chopped parsley. Mix all ingredients together and put in refrigerator 2-3 hours until firm.

Mold fish mixture into flat cakes, coat them in egg and bread crumbs and fry until golden brown in butter or margarine. Garnish with lemon, and serve with Dijon mustard, salad, pickles, and your favorite bread and spread.

Bob and Noreen Owens
Spokane, Washington

Spicy Carp Cakes

3-4 lbs. carp fillets
2 cups Ritz crackers, crushed
3 tsp. fish seasoning mix, more or less to taste
1 tsp. ground black pepper
1 egg
½ tsp. Tabasco sauce
canola oil for frying

Poach carp fillets until fish flakes easily with a fork. Let cool. Remove and discard strong, dark parts of fish. Chop into bitesized pieces.

In a large bowl, mix carp and remaining ingredients thoroughly. Heat ¼" canola oil in skillet until hot. Form cakes and fry until fillets are well browned, about 4 minutes on each side. Remove cakes from skillet and place on paper towels to absorb excess oil.

Elvin M. Rose
Ranson, West Virginia

Cajun Catfish

1 lb. catfish cut in strips or chunks
prepared mustard
1 cup flour
1 cup cornmeal
1 T. Cajun seasoning
1 T. salt
½ tsp. pepper
grease for deep frying

Put fish in a bowl and add enough mustard to completely coat on all sides. Set aside (can be refrigerated in covered container for several hours).

Mix remaining ingredients (except grease) in plastic bag. Heat grease. Put fish in bag and coat with flour mixture. Deep fat fry until brown and tender. Do not overcook. This tastes a lot like shrimp. We serve it with cocktail sauce. Potato chunks can also be coated with flour mix and fried in same pot.

Cheryl Curtis
Olsburg, Kansas

Blackened Catfish

6 catfish fillets
1 T. paprika
2½ tsp. salt
1 tsp. onion powder
1 tsp. garlic powder
¾ tsp. black pepper

¾ tsp. white pepper
½ tsp. oregano
½ tsp. thyme
1 cup butter, melted
1 lemon, cut in wedges

Heat a large skillet on an outdoor grill at medium-high heat until a white ash is visible on the skillet bottom. Mix all seasonings in a shallow dish or plate. Put fillets in the melted butter. Remove and sprinkle mixed seasoning on both sides of fillets and pat down by hand. Put fillets in hot skillet and sprinkle additional seasoning over top of fillets. Cook 2-3 minutes on both sides until chared. Serve with a squeeze of lemon juice.

Daryl Hoffman
Harvey, North Dakota

Catfish a la Story

4 catfish fillets
¼ cup milk
1 egg
⅓ cup flour
½ tsp. salt
½ tsp. cayenne pepper

½ cup butter
¼ cup vegetable oil
2 T. lemon juice
½ tsp. Worcestershire sauce
2 T. chopped parsley

In shallow bowl, combine milk and egg. In another bowl, combine flour, salt and cayenne pepper. Dip catfish in milk mixture, then in flour mixture, shaking off excess.

Heat 4 tablespoons butter and all of the oil in large skillet. Add catfish and cook until golden brown, turning only once.

Meanwhile, melt remaining 4 tablespoons butter. Add lemon juice, parsley, and Worcestershire sauce. Transfer fish to plate and pour butter sauce over top.

Ronnie Story
Jones, Oklahoma

Catfish Jerky

1 lb. channel catfish fillets
1 3.5-oz. bottle liquid smoke
1 10-oz. bottle soy sauce

Mix liquid smoke and soy sauce together. Cut catfish in ¾" strips. Soak fish in liquid smoke and soy sauce for 20 minutes.

Place in dehydrator for about 36 hours.

Ruel Long
Atoka, Oklahoma

Catfish Roll-Ups

8 catfish fillets
1 qt. cooking oil for deep frying
1 large egg
½ lb. white crab, picked clean
  of shells
1 cup onion, finely chopped
½ tsp. peanut oil
½ cup plain bread crumbs
4 strips bacon
1 cup corn flour

1 cup all-purpose flour
1 tsp. onion powder
  ground cayenne pepper to taste
  salt to taste

Fill a deep pot about half full with cooking oil. Preheat to 375 degrees. In a small mixing bowl, beat the egg. Then mix in crabmeat, onions, peanut oil and bread crumbs. Spread 2 tablespoons of this dressing on each of the fillets, then roll up and wrap the fillet with a bacon strip, securing it with a toothpick.

Mix the corn flour, flour, onion powder, cayenne pepper, and salt together in a small mixing bowl and dredge the roll-ups. Fry in cooking oil for 4-6 minutes.

James Miller
North Edwards, California

Paul Gonzales

Grilled Catfish

  5 lb. catfish, whole
¼ cup olive oil or nonfat cooking spray
½ tsp. garlic powder
½ tsp. onion salt
½ tsp. lemon pepper
½ tsp. cinnamon
  1 cup cedar chips

Clean and skin fish. Sprinkle with garlic powder, onion salt and lemon pepper.

Place soaked cedar chips over white medium-hot charcoals. Grill fish on well-oiled grill for 10-15 minutes. Sprinkle cinnamon over fish and grill another 5-10 minutes or until fish flakes when tested with fork.

Serve with brown rice and vegetables.

Paul Gonzales
San Jose, California

Catfish with Dill Sauce

2 lbs. catfish fillets
   seasoned flour
2 eggs, beaten
¾ cup vegetable oil
   dill sauce

Dust fillets with seasoned flour. Dip in egg, then in flour again. Heat oil in large fry pan until very hot. Add fish and saute until golden on both sides (7-10 minutes). Remove to heated platter. Spoon dill sauce (see below) over fish fillets and garnish with lemon wedges and parsley. Makes 4-6 servings.

Dill Sauce

¼ cup butter
1 T. lemon juice
2 tsp. chopped dill
¼ cup brown sauce (see below)

Heat butter and lemon juice. Add dill, stir in brown sauce. Cook and stir until heated through and blended.

Brown Sauce

2 cubes beef bouillon
2½ cups boiling water
2 sprigs parsley
¼ cup butter or margarine
6 T. flour
1 tsp. soy sauce

Dissolve bouillon cubes in boiling water and add parsley. Simmer 10 minutes. Remove parsley and return to boil. In a separate pan, melt butter and stir in flour to make a thick paste. Add this mixture to boiling bouillon. Add soy sauce, and stir until sauce has reached a medium consistency. Refrigerate extra sauce and serve, after reheating, as a garnish with other seafoods.

B. Charles Hoette
Downers Grove, Illinois

Charcoal Grilled Catfish

1 catfish, any size
  butter, melted
  fresh garlic, minced
  seasoning to taste

Clean and skin your catch. Put butter and garlic in body cavity. Wrap in aluminum foil and place on hot grill for about 10 minutes on first side. Flip and cook for about 3-5 minutes more. Remove from grill, open foil, and season to taste.

Jerry Baylow
Leechburg, Pennsylvania

Hot Fried Cajun Catfish

10-12 catfish fillets
  3 eggs
  1 cup cornmeal
  2 T. hot Cajun powder or cayenne pepper
    onion powder
    onions, fried
    bell peppers strips, fried

Beat eggs in a bowl. Combine cornmeal and Cajun powder. Dip fillets in egg and dredge through cornmeal. Fry in a hot pan and sprinkle with onion powder.

Serve hot, smothered with fried onions and bell peppers. Serve with wine or beer.

Justin Watkins
Wickes, Arkansas

Lazy Baked Fish

4 large catfish fillets
1 bottle zesty Italian dressing

Line a deep pan with aluminum foil. Put fish in pan. Pour dressing over fish fillets until it comes half way up the fish. Bake, uncovered, at 250 degrees about 15 minutes. Turn and bake another 15 minutes until meat comes apart. Salt and pepper to taste

Howard H. Hixson
Harrodsburg, Kentucky

Wisker Stew

6 lbs. catfish fillets
2 qts. water
2 tsp. salt
1½ pints milk
2 potatoes, cut in small cubes
2 T. butter
¼ cup onion
2 T. parsley or chives
¼ tsp. salt
¼ tsp. pepper
⅛ tsp. red pepper

Boil fish in salted water 5 minutes. Remove from heat and drain water. Add all other ingredients. Cook over low heat until potatoes are done. Do not boil. Great "cold-day" food.

Gordon Bender
Dewitt, Iowa

Catfish Pot-au-Feu

The little blond girl down the block asked the name of this dish when passing her plate back for her third helping - we always double this recipe to insure leftovers. When she heard the name she knew she had just eaten "a pot of furry catfish."

She left the table with a horrified look at our catfish and a muttered "poor kitty." It took ten minutes and chocolate cake to get her back to the table and each time she eats here she's careful to ask what's what before she lifts her fork.

Under any name catfish pot-au-feu is both delicious and the kind of dish that particularly suits a cold winter day. Serve it in bowls and pass crusty French bread if you like. We also like to pass Aioli, a garlic-powered home-made French-style mayonnaise. We've made this dish with various bullheads and cats. Best, to our taste, are channel cats from a cold water stream.

- 4 lbs. cat fillets
- 6 cups chicken broth or stock
- 1 cup white wine
- 1 tsp. tarragon
- 8 small red potatoes
- 4 small carrots, cut in half
- 4 medium leeks, or two onions, quartered

Boil the stock, wine and tarragon. Reduce heat, add potatoes and carrots and simmer 8-10 minutes. Then add onions or leeks and simmer about 10 minutes more or until vegetables are tender, remove them from the stock and keep covered and warm.

Lower the fillets into the stock and cook about ten minutes or until opaque all the way through. Carefully remove fish with a slotted spoon and place each piece in a soup bowl. Turn soup back to high. Add red potatoes, carrot pieces and leeks or onions to each bowl. Pour hot soup over the top and serve.

Variations: A crunchy slice of French Bread under the fish in the bowl isn't bad. You can toast the bread on one side in the broiler, then paint the uncooked side with olive oil, pepper and a sprinkle of Parmesan cheese. Toast that side and serve it in the bowl. We pass grated cheese with this as well.

Lou Bignami
Moscow, Idaho

Buttermilk Fried Catfish

The shack on the levee didn't look like much, but the girth of the lady who cooked testified to her food.

The catfish that arrived on a metal tray big enough to hold twenty Big Macs was golden brown, huge and gone faster than a teenager at chore time.

Speed was the trick. First, a live catfish held in the river and "whomped," was skinned with the old "nail on the wall" system and dumped into a COLD batter of buttermilk and seasoned flour. Then she popped the cat into a fry pot full of hot oil that was so big a large fish couldn't reduce the temperature below 350 degrees and make it taste oily.

Buttermilk used to be a problem. Now it comes powdered for pancakes and you can't tell the difference. So in camp we use the same pancake mix for cats and flapjacks.

2-3 lbs. catfish fillets
  Cooking oil
  2 cups buttermilk pancake mix
  1 tsp. white pepper
  ¼ tsp. cayenne pepper
  ½ tsp. salt
1-2 cups buttermilk
  Sliced lemon for garnish.

Combine pancake mix, seasonings and thin with buttermilk. Place in the refrigerator to chill.

Heat oil in a fryer, Dutch oven or deep pot to about 375 degrees. Use a thermometer or a test cube of fish that should brown in 60 seconds. Dip the catfish fillets into cold batter and then into the oil. Cook about ten minutes per side. Drain on a rack over paper towels and serve at once (don't put fish directly on paper towels they may loose a bit of that lovely crispy texture).

Lou Bignami
Moscow, Idaho

Easy Catfish Casserole

This takes no more than 5 minutes to set up if you have cooked rice and catfish on hand. Or, make it a day ahead of time and keep it in the refrigerator until you're ready to cook it. If you take it from the fridge straight to the oven, cook for 45 minutes instead of half an hour.

1 lb. of cooked catfish in pieces
3 T. butter
3 T. flour
1 T. salt
1 T. oregano
½ T. marjoram
    dash pepper
1½ cups cooked rice
1½ cups tomato juice
¼ onion, grated
1 green pepper, diced
⅔ cup mayonnaise

Heat oven to 400 degrees. Melt butter, add flour and stir to a paste or roux over medium heat until not quite golden bown. Stir in tomato juice and cook until sauce thickens. Add remaining ingredients, stir and pour into a casserole dish. Top with bread crumbs or parmesan cheese. Bake 20-30 minutes.

Lou Bignami
Moscow, Idaho

Catfish on Grass

This dish suits summer nights, or dinners on the boat, as it only takes one pan. It's a dandy way to introduce kids to spinach, too.

1½ lbs. catfish fillets in 1-inch cubes
 4 bacon slices
 ½ cup onion, finely slivered (Valdosta or mild red)
 2 qts. fresh spinach
 2 T. red wine vinegar
2-4 tsp. sugar

Cook bacon in a Dutch oven over medium-high heat until it browns and crisps. Drain bacon on paper, crumble and reserve.

Add onion and catfish pieces to bacon fat and brown lightly. Remove catfish when it's opaque and reserve in a warm spot.

Put the spinach into the pot with the crumbled bacon and stir until spinach wilts, about 4-5 minutes. Sprinkle on vinegar and sugar to taste. Toss lightly.

Place "grass" on platter and top with catfish. Serves four as dinner and eight as a fish course or "salad."

Lou Bignami
Moscow, Idaho

Blackened Catfish

You can eat anything "blackened" as all you really taste is the burned butter. So save this dish for catfish that come from muddy, still waters and seem to lack the taste and texture of cold water channel cats. It's a very easy dish to do outside, and you can do it indoors if you disconnect the smoke alarm and someone else gets the grease off the kitchen ceiling.

7-8 lbs. catfish fillets
  2 tsp. paprika
  ¼ tsp. dry basil leaves
  ¼ tsp. thyme
  6 bay leaves, crushed
  ½ tsp. garlic powder
  2 T. salt
  ¼ tsp. pepper
  ¼ tsp. cayenne pepper
  ¼ tsp. white pepper
  2 cubes butter

Pat fillets dry and chill one hour in the refrigerator. Combine remaining ingredients except butter in a bowl. Sprinkle seasonings on both sides of each fillet and place them on waxed paper. Melt butter in a separate pan.

Heat a cast-iron skillet or Dutch oven until the bottom is nearly red hot. Dip fillets in the melted butter to coat them and immediately drop them into the hot skillet or Dutch oven. Cook just 30-40 seconds or until dark brown, then flip and cook the other side 30-40 seconds.

NOTE: the fillets will sputter and smoke so wise cooks prepare this recipe outdoors on a camp stove. Remove fillets from your blackened pan and serve topped with any leftover melted butter.

Lou Bignami
Moscow, Idaho

Crisp Lemon Crappies

1 stringer of crappies, cleaned
2-3 eggs, beaten
2 tsp. lemon juice

cornmeal
flour
lemon pepper

Wash crappies and dry with paper towel. Dip in mixture of beaten eggs and lemon juice. Roll in cornmeal mixed with a little flour. Sprinkle with lemon pepper seasoning and fry until golden brown.

Shirley Bos
Rock Valley, Iowa

Crispy Fish Bake

1½ lbs. crappie fillets
2½ T. margarine, melted
2½ T. vegetable oil

crisp coating (recipe below)
1 egg
¼ cup milk

Crisp Coating

3 cups corn flakes, crushed
2 T. sesame seeds
1 tsp. dry parsley, crushed
1 tsp. paprika
¼ tsp. salt

¼ tsp. dry mustard
¼ tsp. celery salt
¼ tsp. onion salt
¼ tsp. black pepper

Preheat oven to 500 degrees. Combine margarine and oil on large baking sheet with raised sides. Place sheet in oven until hot.

Mix all ingredients for crisp coating in a plastic bag. Set aside. In a shallow dish, beat egg and milk until blended.

Rinse fish; pat dry with paper towel. Dip each fillet in milk mixture. Put 1 fillet in coating bag and shake to coat. Arrange on baking sheet, turning to coat with oil mixture. Bake 7-10 minutes until fish flakes when tested with a fork.

Mrs. Lonnie Willis
Newalla, Oklahoma

Crunchy Crappie

8 large crappie fillets
½ cup flour
1 tsp. salt
½ tsp. black pepper
2 eggs
1 cup crushed potato chips

Combine flour, salt and pepper in a bowl. Beat eggs in a different bowl. Put chips in a third bowl. Lightly coat both sides of fillets with the flour mixture. Then dip in eggs, allowing excess to drip off. Next, dredge in the chips, pressing the coating into the fillets. Fry fillets in hot oil until golden brown.

Dennis Arch
Larimer, Pennsylvania

Fish Casserole

12 crappie fillets
2 large potatoes, sliced
2 tomatoes, sliced thin
1 green pepper, sliced thin
1 T. oil
½ cup bread crumbs or crushed potato chips

Lightly grease a 2-quart casserole. Layer ingredients in following order: potatoes, tomatoes, green pepper, fish. Repeat layers, finishing with fish. Brush oil over fish and cover with bread crumbs or crushed potato chips. Bake, covered, for 45 minutes at 350 degrees. Remove cover and bake another 10 minutes.

Peter Todaro
Buffalo, New York

Fried Crappie Fingers with Dipping Sauce

3 lbs. crappie fillets, cut into bite-sized fingers
2 cups self-rising cornmeal
2 T. all-purpose flour
   black pepper to taste
4 eggs, beaten
   vegetable oil

Heat oil in a large skillet or a fryer to 350 degrees. Combine cornmeal, flour and pepper in a shallow bowl. Beat eggs in another bowl. Dry fillets on paper towels.

Dredge fillets in eggs, then cornmeal mixture, back in eggs and then back in cornmeal. Let the coated fillets rest for a few minutes before frying. Fry to a golden brown.

The best part is the Red Dipping Sauce you serve with the fried crappie fingers. Here's how you make it:

Red Dipping Sauce

1½ cups ketchup
  2 T. brown sugar
  2 T. Worcestershire sauce
  1 tsp. dry mustard
 ½ cup Jack Daniels Whiskey

Mix ketchup, brown sugar, Worcestershire sauce and dry mustard in a small saucepan. Bring to a boil, stirring occasionally. Stir in whiskey and simmer for 5 minutes. Refrigerate until serving time and serve with the crappie fingers.

Norma Blank
Shawano, Wisconsin

Quick Crappies & Gills

crappie or bluegill fillets
vegetable oil
flour
equal parts garlic powder, garlic salt and lemon pepper
salt

Cover bottom of frying pan with vegetable oil. Heat until oil begins to smoke. Next, put enough flour on a plate so you'll be able to dust all your fillets. Put the floured fillets into the hot, greased pan. Sprinkle with some seasoning and a little salt.

Depending on the size of your fillets, I suggest 3-4 minutes on a side. Turn, then re-season. You don't want mushy fish, so cook until firm and flaky. Drain on a paper towel.

John Wahl
Waterloo, Iowa

Krispie Crappie

This recipe works particularly well with kids who don't much like fish. We suspect it got started as a way to use stale breakfast food as it works great with Rice Krispies, Corn Flakes, etc.

2 lbs. crappie fillets
1 cube butter
1 teaspoon garlic powder
¼ tsp. salt
⅛ tsp. pepper
3 cups Rice Krispies, finely crushed

Rinse fillets and pat dry. Melt butter in a saucepan over low heat, stir in garlic powder, salt and pepper. Dip fillets into butter mixture; then roll in Rice Krispies. Bake on a foil-lined cookie sheet for 25 minutes in a 375 degree oven or until brown and fish flakes with a fork.

Lou Bignami
Moscow, Idaho

Baked Fillet of Flounder

1½ lbs. fresh flounder fillets (about ½-inch thick)
2 cups rice, brown or white, cooked
6 slices bacon, freshly cooked and chopped
6 plum tomatoes, peeled and diced
⅓ cup fresh onion, diced
5 oz. milk
1 10¾ oz. can cream of mushroom soup
pepper to taste
1 cup shredded mild longhorn-style Colby cheese
1 pinch sweet basil

In 9" x 13" baking dish, mix rice and bacon and allow to cool. Mix tomatoes and onion in small bowl. Mix milk with mushroom soup and warm in a pan until creamy. Add half the soup to rice mixture, stir and spread evenly in bottom of baking dish.

Arrange fillets over rice and soup mixture. Lightly pepper flounder fillets. Spread diced tomato and onion over flounder evenly. Spoon remaining soup over fillets and tomato mixture. Spread cheese evenly on top. Sprinkle with a pinch of sweet basil. Bake at 375 degrees for about 20 minutes.

This recipe works equally well with any boneless fillets, although cooking times may vary, depending on the thickness of the fillets.

Bruce Manning
Chester Springs, Pennsylvania

Deep-Fried Flounder

2 lbs. flounder fillets
cooking oil
1 cup flour
1½ tsp. salt
1 tsp. pepper
2 eggs, beaten
1 cup bread crumbs

Heat cooking oil (3-5 inches deep) in fryer to 375 degrees. Cut fillets into serving-sized pieces. Stir flour, salt and pepper together and coat flounder in flour mixture. Dip in eggs, and coat with bread crumbs. Fry until golden brown. Serve with tartar sauce and lemon wedges.

Chris Hodson
Hopewell, Virginia

Grouper de Franco

1 grouper fillet (about 1-inch thick works best)
flour
1 egg
½ cup milk
bread crumbs to coat fillet

2 T. butter
1 pkg. sliced mushrooms, fresh
2 cloves garlic, sliced
1 pkg. prepared Hollandaise sauce (need to add one stick of butter)

Beat egg and mix with milk. Dredge fillet through flour and shake. Dip in egg/milk mixture. Shake in bag with bread crumbs. In a skillet, melt butter and brown fillet lightly on either side. Do not thoroughly cook.

At the same time, saute sliced mushrooms in butter with garlic. Place browned fillet on broiler pan. Top with mushrooms. Ladle some hollandaise on top. Bake at 350 degrees until done. Do not overcook.

Note: This recipe was originally developed for grouper butis also delicious with snook, dolphin, and even kingfish steaks.

Rick Sewell
Port St. Lucie, Florida

Tom Gutting

Baked Halibut and Rice

2 lbs. halibut fillets
garlic salt
fresh ground pepper
2 large onions, thinly sliced
4-6 cups cooked rice, cold

1 fresh ginger root, thinly sliced
¼ cup butter

If required, cut fillets into ½" thickness. Liberally sprinkle with garlic salt and pepper to taste. Place half the onions and several pieces of ginger root on a sheet of aluminum foil. Cover onions with half of halibut fillets and top with several pats of butter. Place cooked rice on top of fillets. Put remaining fillets topped with butter over the rice. Cover with rest of onions and ginger root. Wrap aluminum foil around the entire combination. Bake at 350 degrees for about 45 minutes.

Tom Gutting
Moorpark, California

Walt Harrington

Walt's Easy Halibut

halibut fillets
milk or beaten eggs
flour or bread crumbs

In preparing my halibut, I find the most important thing is to be sure the fillets are thin enough. I like to cut my fillets about 1" thick. Then all I do is dip them in milk or beaten egg, put them in a bag of either flour or bread crumbs and shake till covered.

Place the fillets in a deep-fat fryer with clean, hot fat. Usually when they float and turn golden brown, they're done. If not all eaten hot, they make great cold snacks the next day.

Walt Harrington
Eutawville, South Carolina

Baked Halibut with Shrimp

4-6 lbs. halibut, fresh or frozen
 2 cans cream of celery soup
 1 lb. popcorn shrimp, frozen
    salt, pepper and garlic powder to taste

Preheat oven to 350 degrees. Combine all ingredients in 8-inch square glass baking dish, leaving shrimp frozen. Cover dish with foil and bake 1 hour or until fish flakes and is tender. Turn oven down to 300 degrees if meat is cooking too fast. Soup will make a gravy. Serve with rice.

Tom Bennett
North Pole, Arkansas

Halibut Parmesan

 1 lb. halibut fillets
 ¼ cup onion, chopped
 1 tsp. oil
 ¼ cup mayonnaise
 ¼ cup Parmesan cheese, grated
 2 T. lemon juice
 1 tsp. Worcestershire sauce
 ½ tsp. paprika
 1 T. fresh, chopped parsley

Saute onion in oil and spoon into baking dish. Put fish on top of onions. Mix mayonnaise, Parmesan, lemon juice, Worcestershire sauce, paprika and parsley. Spread over top of fish. Bake at 350 degrees for 30 minutes.

Wallace Brandt
Concord, California

Northwest-Style Halibut

    2 lbs. halibut steaks or fillets
    ½ cup flour
    1 tsp. salt
    ¼ tsp. pepper
       pinch of nutmeg
    ¼ cup melted butter
    1½ cup milk
    ⅓ cup Parmesan cheese, grated
    ½ tsp. Worcestershire sauce
    2 pkgs. frozen chopped spinach, thawed and well drained
       paprika

Preheat oven to 350 degrees. Remove skin and bones from fish and cut into serving-sized pieces.

Blend flour, salt, pepper, nutmeg and butter in a small pan. Gradually stir in milk to make a white sauce. Bring to a boil, stirring constantly. Add Parmesan and Worcestershire sauce.

Combine spinach with half the sauce and spread in bottom of greased shallow baking dish. Arrange fish pieces over spinach. Pour remaining sauce over fish. Sprinkle with paprika and bake 20-25 minutes or until fish flakes easily when tested with a fork.

Rob Tumpach
Kirkland, Washington

Cajun King Mackerel

1 King mackerel, dressed and cut into 1-inch steaks
Italian salad dressing
blackening spice
salsa, thick and chunky style
Monterey Jack or hot pepper cheese, shredded

Soak mackerel in ice water for 1-2 hours. Drain and pat dry. Marinate steaks in plenty of Italian dressing for 4-6 hours. Remove steaks from dressing, shake off excess and heavily coat with blackening spice.

Prepare coals for grilling. Charcoal should be hot with ample amount of mesquite chunks or chips. Grill 90 minutes to 2 hours per side. Douse coals with water, place foil tent over grill and allow steaks to steam until fire goes out. Remove steaks to baking sheet. Top each steak with 1-2 tablespoons salsa and add cheese. Place in broiler until cheese is melted. Serve with red beans and rice.

Tim Rola
St. Louis, Missouri

Jack Mackerel Cakes

1 fresh mackerel, ground coarsely
1 cup onions, chopped
1 cup celery, chopped
1 egg
3 slices fresh bread
salt and pepper

Put fish in bowl. Add onions, celery, and egg. Crumble bread into bowl and add salt and pepper. Mix all ingredients and form into patties. Fry until brown.

Christine Goldsborough
Harrisville, West Virginia

Mother-in-Law's Muskie

1 muskie, cleaned and cut into 1½ inch steaks

Mix equal amounts of:

> ketchup
> lemon-lime soda
> Italian dressing

Marinate fish in the ketchup, soda and dressing marinade for 12 hours or overnight. Cook on charcoal grill, basting occasionally with sauce.

Jack Nickol
McHenry, Illinois

Broiled Perch with Lime-Ginger Butter

4 perch fillets, about 6 oz. each
  salt and pepper
5 T. lime-ginger butter (see recipe below)
  parsley, chopped fresh

Lime Ginger Butter

½ stick butter at room temperature
2 tsp. grated lime zest
2 tsp. ground ginger
½ tsp. salt
  pepper to taste

Preheat broiler. Lightly season fillets with salt and pepper and broil until cooked throughout, about 5 minutes.

Divide butter evenly and spread over top of fillets. Sprinkle with parsley and serve.

Jerry Solberg
Weyauwega, Wisconsin

Chipper Perch

12 perch fillets
1 cup French dressing
12 oz. potato chips, crushed
8 oz. cheddar cheese, shredded
1 T. red pepper (optional)

Separate fillets and dip them in dressing. Place on sheet pan, skin side down.

Combine chips and cheese; sprinkle over fish. Top with red pepper if desired. Bake at 350 degrees for 10 minutes or until fish flakes easily. Makes 6 servings.

Daniel Kuenne
Wausau, Wisconsin

Delicious Fish Stew

1 lb. perch
1 small onion, chopped
1 clove garlic, mashed
1 T. olive oil
3 small tomatoes, diced
1 green or red pepper, diced
1 cup fresh cucumber, peeled
    and diced

$\frac{1}{2}$ tsp. dried basil leaves
$\frac{1}{4}$ tsp. dried oregano
1 cup water
$\frac{1}{2}$ tsp. salt
$\frac{1}{8}$ tsp pepper

Cut fish into 1" cubes.

In Dutch oven, saute onion and garlic in oil until tender. Add tomatoes, sweet pepper, cucumber, basil and oregano. Saute 2 minutes. Add water and heat to simmering. Add fish. Cook 10-15 minutes or until fish is just tender. Add salt and pepper. Heat 2 more minutes. Serve with with toasted, buttered garlic bread.

Bryon Lasher
Union City, Pennsylvania

Lemon Parsley Panfish

perch fillets
1 lemon
1 bunch parsley, fresh
2 cups flour
salt and pepper
½ stick butter or margarine
white wine

Wash and dry lemon. Grate rind to remove zest and set aside in a small dish. Chop one bunch of parsley leaves. Set aside in another small dish. Cut lemon into wedges. In a large bowl, combine flour, salt and pepper.

In frying pan on low to medium heat, melt butter or margarine. Coat fish with flour mixture and put in pan. Sprinkle with parsley and lemon peel and cook 1 minute. Flip fish over and squeeze juice of 2 lemon wedges. Pour 2 ounces white wine over fish and cook until tender and flaky.

Ron Hisey
Lake Geneva, Wisconsin

Perch Cocktail

8 perch, filleted and boned
1½ celery stalks, diced
1-2 slices onion, diced
2 tsp. Worcestershire sauce
½ cup hot catsup or ¼ cup hot catsup and ¼ cup regular catsup
salt and pepper to taste

Boil fish for 5-6 minutes. Drain and chill in freezer. After chilled, break into small pieces.

Mix all remaining ingredients and chill. Serve as you would shrimp cocktail.

Edward L. Burdette
Great Falls, Montana

Perch Fillets in Beer Batter

25 perch, 8 inches long
 2 cups buttermilk pancake mix
 1 can beer
    salt and pepper to taste
    brown paper bag

Fillet fish (both sides of back bone) and take out rib cage. Remove skin. Rinse.

Pour pancake mix in bowl and add enough beer to make a thick, soupy batter. Dip fillets in batter. Coat well. Deep fry to golden brown. Shake off excess oil as you remove fish. Drop fish in brown paper bag to soak up rest of oil and keep fish warm. Serve with a loaf of bread, chowder or salad, and maybe a bottle of wine.

Howard Elliott
Holiday, Florida

Perch-Potato Casserole

 3 lbs. boiled perch, boned and flaked
¼ cup butter
 2 T. flour
 2 cups milk
 2 cups soft bread crumbs
 2 cups potatoes, sliced
 2 onions, medium size, sliced
    salt and pepper to taste

In saucepan over medium heat, make a white sauce by blending 2 tablespoons butter with flour. Add milk, stirring constantly, until thickened.

Reserve small amount of crumbs for topping. Place half the fish, potatoes, onions and remaining crumbs in layers in greased 2-quart casserole dish. Add seasonings and 1 cup of the white sauce. Repeat. Top with reserved crumbs. Dot with remaining butter. Bake in 325 degree oven for 1 hour.

Charles Kirby
Sweet Springs, Missouri

Poor Man's Shrimp

perch
cocktail sauce

Clean and gut perch. It is not necessary to scale them. Boil until flesh is white and firm, about 5 minutes. Remove from boiling water and drop in large bowl of ice water. The best fish curls off the carcass when you drop it in ice water. Dip fish in cocktail sauce.

Stephen Earley
Andover, Massachusetts

Perch Vera Cruz

A south of the border treat that's equally good with bass or catfish fillets. Just adjust cooking times.

1¼ lbs. perch fillets	2½ cups chopped tomatoes
5 T. butter	¼ tsp. salt
1 garlic minced	¼ tsp. pepper
½ cup chopped onion	1 tsp. sugar
3 T. chopped celery	1 tsp. mild, chili powder
2 T. finely chopped	½ tsp. dried thyme leaves
bell pepper	2 T. fresh minced parsley
1½ T. flour	

Heat oven to 350 degrees. Grease a shallow baking pan with one tablespoon butter. Arrange the fillets side by side in the pan.

In skillet, melt the remaining butter over medium heat and cook the garlic, onion, celery and bell pepper until tender. Stir in flour and cook until lightly brown. Add the tomatoes, salt, pepper, sugar, thyme and parsley. Bring to a boil, remove from heat and pour over the fish fillets. Bake 20-30 minutes or until the fish flakes.

Sauce can be prepared ahead, then brought back to a boil before it's added to the fish and baked.

Lou Bignami
Moscow, Idaho

Grilled Pickerel

- 2 lbs. pickerel fillets
- 1 tsp. salt
- 1 tsp. pepper
- 4 tsp. butter
- 1 tsp. lemon juice
- 1 tsp. Lawry's seasoning salt

Place fillets on aluminum foil and cover with all other ingredients. Wrap foil securely around fish and place directly on the grill. Cook until you can touch fillets with a fork and meat falls apart.

Jeff Ball
Richmond, Virginia

Bad River Pickerel Casserole

- 4-8 large pickerel fillets
- 1 can cream of mushroom soup
- ¼ tsp. salt
- ¼ tsp. pepper
- ¼ tsp. garlic salt or powder
- ½ cup French white wine (or California in a pinch)
- 2 T. butter
- 1 T. parsley
- ½ cup milk
- 1 can mushrooms or ½ lb. fresh sliced
- 1 T. hot sauce

R. Bruce Douglas

Lay out fillets in baking dish or deep pot. Mix soup, mushrooms, wine, milk and seasonings. Pour over fish and spread evenly. Place butter and green stuff evenly over fish. Put in oven and cook for 25-30 minutes at 325-350 degrees.

R. Bruce Douglas
Newmarket, Ontario

Bryan's Boneless Northern Pike

2-5 lb. northern pike, bones removed
5 cups milk
1 10-oz. can tomato sauce
1 green pepper, diced
1 small onion, diced
1 clove fresh garlic, diced
  butter
  salt and pepper to taste

If fish is frozen, remove dark-colored meat (this will taste fishy). Cut into fillets and soak in milk for 1 hour. Rinse thoroughly and dry on paper towels. Using aluminum foil, make a pan with sides (no holes). Arrange fillets in pan. Add a pat of butter to each fillet. Top with green pepper, onion, garlic, tomato sauce and salt and pepper. Place another sheet of foil over your pan.

Place on grill for 30 minutes. Remove and poke a hole in one end and drain juices (this makes a great gravy). Place back on grill for 5-8 minutes to firm up the meat. Fish can also be baked in a 350-degree oven for 30 minutes, drained, and heated for 5-8 minutes longer.

Robert Bryan
Milaca, Minnesota

Grilled Fish Fillets

1 lb. pike
2 tsp. olive oil
  pinch fresh or dried thyme
  pinch fresh or dried fennel
2 fresh lemons, cut into wedges.

Rub fish with olive oil. Season with spices. Oil grill and cook fish 3-4 inches above coals, turning once. Serve with fresh lemon.

Jerry Solberg
Wayauwega, Wisconsin

Hugh Lyberg

Hugh Lyberg's Favorite Fish Recipe

1 fish, fresh from lake
1 egg from a big white chicken
1 stick butter, fresh from refrigerator
1 pkg. saltine crackers, from box in cupboard
½ cup milk, fresh from plastic cow in refrigerator

Put egg and milk in bowl and beat them silly. Put saltines on waxed paper and crush until powderized or until you feel better about losing that 10 pound walleye you had right next to the boat.

Melt butter in frying pan at medium heat. If you start developing spots from hot butter burns, turn down to medium.

Take your fish fillet, freed of bones and scales, and dip it in the beaten egg and milk mixture. Then, roll the fish in the crackers and place in frying pan. Repeat for all fillets. As you watch fish turn a golden brown on both sides, you feel that it was a good day fishing. As you taste the fish, you know it was a good day fishing. ENJOY!

Hugh Lyberg
Eau Claire, Wisconsin

Northern Pike Patties

5 lbs. northern pike, ground
1 lb. pork sausage, ground
2 large onions, chopped
3-4 eggs
    salt and pepper to taste
    garlic, sage, onion powder or other favorite spices to taste

Mix all ingredients as if making meatloaf. Make into patties. If mixture is too dry, add enough milk for correct consistency.

To prepared, deep-fat fry, pan fry or bake.

Bill Schoenberg
Hancock, Minnesota

Paprika Fish Fillets

6-8 pike fillets
    butter or olive oil
3 large onions, sliced
1 green pepper, sliced
2 T. paprika
3 T. water

Steam fillets until they flake when tested with a fork. Saute onions in butter or olive oil. Add rest of ingredients and heat until warm. Pour over steamed fish.

Jerry Solberg
Weyauwega, Wisconsin

Pickled Northern Pike

2 lb. northern pike fillets cut into 1-inch pieces.
1 cup pickling salt
4 cups water
  white vinegar

Place fish in glass bowl. Prepare brine by combine pickling salt and water. Pour over fish and refrigerate overnight. Fish will be "firmed up" from the salt. Wash fish and soak in white vinegar 3-4 days (this virtually dissolves the 'y' bones). Drain, rinse, and place in jars along with pickling solution given below.

2 cups vinegar
1¾ cups sugar

In each jar, along with fish, add:

⅓ onion, chopped or sliced
⅓ lemon, thinly sliced
1 T. whole mustard seed
4 bay leaves
5-6 whole cloves
1 T. whole peppercorns
5-6 small red peppers, fresh or dried.

Pour pickling solution over all, cover and store in refrigerator for at least a week to allow flavors to blend.

(Prepared for 1-pint Mason jars with lids. Number of jars needed depends on amount of fish).

Ed Kveton
Warrenville, Illinois

David Kauzlarich

Southern Fried Northern Pike

     pike fillets
½ cup milk
¾ cup cornmeal
½ cup flour
     seasoning salt
     garlic salt
     onion salt
     lemon pepper seasoning (if desired)
     canola or vegetable oil

Heat oil in large skillet. Mix cornmeal, flour, and seasonings. Dip pike into milk, then coat with cornmeal mixture. Place in heated oil. Brown on both sides. Serve hot.

Hint: Be sure oil is very hot before placing fish in it.

David Kauzlarich
Kerkhoven, Minnesota

Simple Spicy Cajun Pike

1 pike, whole
  Cajun seasoning
  Spanish onion, 1 slice for each piece of fish
  margarine

Skin and bone pike. Cut into fillets. Rub fillets with Cajun seasoning and place on baking sheet. Put slice of onion on each fillet and top with a pat of margarine. Bake fish at 350 degrees about 10 minutes on each side, basting occasionally with butter and juices from pan. Place under broiler for about 5 minutes to brown slightly.

Paul Wehrmeister
Manistee, Michigan

Smoked Fish Pike

1 pike, whole, cleaned
½ cup salt
1 cup brown sugar
2 T. lemon or lime juice
1 T. garlic powder

1 T. seafood seasoning
1 qt. hot water
1 qt. cold water

Do not skin or scale fish.

Soak some apple or hickory chips overnight.

Mix salt, brown sugar, lemon or lime juice, garlic powder and seafood seasoning in hot water until sugar is dissolved. Add cold water. Marinate fish in this mixture at least 12 hours (doesn't matter if you marinate longer).

Prepare smoker. After charcoal has reached cooking point, add soaked wood chips. Place fish on top rack of smoker. Pour marinade in water pan of smoker. Smoke fish 2 hours, leaving lid on smoker.

Note: Charcoal impregnated with hickory or mesquite works even better than soaked wood chips.

A. Glenn Maranville, Jr.
Hartville, Ohio

Baked Northern Pike in Sour Cream

1½ lbs. northern pike
    salt
    pepper
  4 red potatoes
  6 slices bacon, cut up
  1 medium onion
  1 medium green pepper
1½ cups sour cream
 ½ cup half-and-half
  2 T. fresh chives, chopped
  1 T. dillweed
 ¼ tsp. tarragon
 ¼ cup fresh parsley, cut up

Boil potatoes in 1 quart of water with a teaspoon of salt in a 2-quart pan. Reduce heat cover and simmer for 30 minutes. Drain and slice potatoes when cool.

Cook bacon in a small skillet until brown. Drain, reserving 2 tablespoons of fat. Cut fish into 2" pieces. Slice onion core and slice green pepper into rings. Set aside.

Heat oven to 325 degrees. Layer potato slices in a 13" x 9" baking pan, pouring reserved bacon fat over potatoes.

Mix sour cream, half-and-half, chives, dillweed, tarragon with ½ teaspoon salt and ⅛ teaspoon of pepper. Cover potatoes with ⅓ of mixture. Layer fish and onion rings over sour cream and potatoes. Spoon on the remaining sour cream. Top with green pepper rings, parsley and bacon. Bake for 1 hour or until fish flakes easily.

Robert Nelson
Duluth, Minnesota

Baked Stuffed Salmon

8-12 salmon, whole
  1 T. salt
  3 T. lemon juice
  1 cup celery, chopped
  1 cup celery leaves, minced
  2 medium onions, thinly sliced
  ¼ cup butter

4 cups whole-wheat or
  rye bread, diced
¼ tsp. thyme or sage
  salt and pepper to taste
2 eggs, lightly beaten
  Sauce (your choice)

Rub cleaned fish inside and out with a mixture of salt and lemon juice. Over medium-low heat, saute the celery, celery leaves and onions in butter until the onions are soft and lightly browned. Pour over the diced bread in a bowl. Blend well. Add the seasonings and eggs. Stir until well mixed. Stuff fish with mixture and tie securely.

Place fish on a well-oiled baking sheet. Bake at 400 degrees for 10 minutes per pound. Serve with hollandaise sauce, tomato sauce or with a sauce made of equal amounts of butter and lemon juice heated together.

Leo G. J. Seffelaar
Broadview, Saskatchewan

Carol's Baked Salmon

  1 lb. salmon fillets
  ½ tsp. salt
    dash pepper
  2 T. margarine or butter, melted
  1 T. lemon juice
  1 tsp. onion, finely chopped
    garlic powder and paprika (optional)

Heat oven to 400 degrees. If fish fillets are large, cut into 3 smaller serving pieces. Arrange fish in ungreased 8" square baking dish. Sprinkle with salt and pepper. Mix margarine, lemon juice, and onion. Drizzle over fish. Bake, uncovered, until fish flakes easily with fork and is opaque in center (25-30 minutes). Sprinkle with garlic powder and paprika if desired.

Carol Shore
Goldendale, Washington

Cheesy Salmon Loaf

12 oz. cooked salmon, chopped
2 eggs
1 cup rolled oats
1 cup grated low-fat mozzarella cheese
¼ cup onion, chopped
1 stalk celery, chopped
1 large carrot, grated
1 T. lemon juice

In large bowl, beat eggs. Stir in rolled oats, salmon, cheese, onion, celery, carrot and lemon juice until well combined. Turn salmon mixture into nonstick or greased 9" x 5" loaf pan. Bake at 350 degrees for about 35 minutes. Allow to stand 5 minutes before slicing.

Leo G. J. Seffelaar
Broadview, Saskatchewan

Creamed Salmon with Peas on Toast

6 oz. cooked salmon, coarsely
    chopped
1½ tsp. dry mustard
½ tsp. salt
⅛ tsp. pepper
½ tsp. paprika
3 tsp. paprika
3 T. flour

2 cups milk
⅓ cup fish stock (or water)
1 egg
2 T. lemon juice
2 T. margarine
1 cup cooked peas
1 tsp. Worcestershire sauce
    toast

Stir seasonings, flour and butter together and heat to combine. Add milk and stock.

Combine eggs and lemon juice, beat slightly with wire whisk. Whip into milk mixture. Cook until sauce thickens. Add salmon, stirring gently. Add Worcestershire sauce and peas. Heat well and serve on toast.

Leo G. J. Seffelaar
Broadview, Saskatchewan

Smoked Salmon

10 lb. salmon steaks or fillets, 1 inch thick
    hickory or mesquite wood chunks
1 gal. water
1 cup molasses or brown sugar
    (or ½ cup of each)
¼ cup Worcestershire sauce

1 T. liquid smoke seasoning
½ cup salt (or to taste)
2 T. pepper
½ T. each: garlic salt, garlic
    pepper, lemon pepper,
    seasoned salt, marjoram,
    rosemary

Combine ingredients (except fish and wood) in large mixing bowl. Add salmon, cover and marinate in refrigerator 24 hours.

Use electric water smoker. Soak wood chunks in water for ½ hour. Place the wood chunks in the smoker near the element but not touching it. Remove the salmon from the mixing bowl and pour marinade into the smoker's water pan. This will boil as the salmon is smoking, keeping the meat moist. Place the salmon in smoker, keeping smaller pieces on the top rack, since they will be ready first. Cover and let smoke for 1½-2½ hours.

After 1 hour, check the top pieces of salmon. If meat flakes when checked with a fork, it is done. Allow the rest to cook to completion. Ingredients and smoking time may vary, depending on individual taste.

Jeff Fearing

Tip: Any small pieces of salmon can be placed in an aluminum foil tray. Simply fold the foil into the shape of a tray and poke holes in the bottom. These small pieces will not take long to cook and you'll be glad you didn't feed them to the cat.

Use this recipe for anything you want to smoke.

Jeff Fearing
Folsom, California

99

Florentine Salmon Steaks

4 salmon steaks
1 envelope sour cream sauce mix
½ cup milk
¼ cup mayonnaise
2 10-oz. pkgs. frozen chopped spinach, thawed
½ tsp. pepper
1 T. butter
¼ cup bread crumbs

Heat oven to 350 degrees. Stir milk into sour cream sauce mix until smooth; let stand for 10 minutes. Blend mayonnaise into sauce mixture. Spread thawed, uncooked spinach on bottom of greased, shallow baking dish. Sprinkle salmon steaks with salt and pepper, dot with butter, and place over spinach. Spread salmon with sour cream mixture and top with bread crumbs. Bake for about 30 minutes.

Samuel T. Gontkovsky
Dave, Florida

Fish Baste

4-6 salmon steaks or fillets
1 stick butter or margarine, melted
8 cloves garlic, finely chopped
2-3 limes (juice and a little pulp)
¾ cup mayonnaise

Melt butter over low heat. Add garlic and allow to soak. Add juice of limes and enough mayonnaise to thicken the mixture so it can be spread on fish fillets without running off.

Baste both sides of fish fillets or steaks (edges too, if ¾" thick or more). Add salt and pepper to taste and cook over bed of charcoal. If desired, add 2 or 3 small chips of mesquite, peach, cherry or pecan wood to fire and cover first 2-3 minutes. Broil 2-5 minutes on each side, depending on thickness of fish.

Dennis Foster
Rialto, California

Fish Mousse with Ginger

1 lb. salmon steaks
3 cups water
½ cup white vermouth
1 small onion, chopped
1 stalk celery, chopped
    salt and pepper to taste
3 T. fresh parsley, chopped
2 T. fresh ginger, grated
1½ envelope unflavored gelatin
¼ lb. smoked salmon (or smoked trout)
¼ cup mayonnaise
2 egg whites
1 T. canned sweet red peppers, diced
½ cup canned or frozen baby shrimp
    lemon slices, marinated ginger, fresh parsley and red pepper slices

Bring water to boil in a large saucepan. Add vermouth, onion, celery, parsley, ginger, salt and pepper. Boil 20 minutes. Add fish. Cook over low heat 10 minutes. Remove fish from pan, reserving cooking liquid. Flake fish with a fork and set aside.

Boil cooking liquid until reduced by half. Cool to lukewarm, then add gelatin without stirring. Let mixture rest for a few minutes, then stir until gelatin dissolves.

Puree cooking liquid, fish, smoked salmon and mayonnaise in a food processor and pour into a large bowl. Stir in red peppers and shrimp. Beat egg whites until stiff, and fold into fish mixture. Pour into a fish-shaped mold and refrigerate several hours. Unmold and garnish with lemon slices, ginger, fresh parsley and red pepper.

Leo G. J. Seffelaar
Broadview, Saskatchewan

Grilled Soy Salmon

   2 lbs. salmon fillets
   1 T. vegetable oil
   1 tsp. soy sauce
   ½ tsp. salt
   ½ tsp. lemon pepper seasoning
   ¼ tsp. garlic powder
   4 T. lemon juice
   4 T. minced parsley

Make marinade of vegetable oil, soy sauce and seasonings. Soak salmon fillets in marinade for about 30 minutes.

Over hot coals or under broiler, cook fish 4-5 minutes per side or 8-10 minutes on one side. Baste fillets with marinade while cooking.

Add lemon juice and parsley to the remaining marinade, heat just to boiling and pour over grilled fish. Garnish with fresh parsley and sliced lemon.

Marie and Clarence Kutscher
Cleveland, Ohio

Ground Salmon

   1 lb. filleted salmon, cut into 1-1½ inch strips
   1 onion, diced

Bring a large pot of salted water to a boil. Add onion and salmon strips. Boil for about 4-5 minutes. Remove salmon from water and drain in a colander with a drip pan in the refrigerator overnight. The salt water draws the fluids from the salmon, and the cooking followed by cooling firms up the meat.

Salmon can now be ground and either used or packaged in freezer bags for use later. The salmon will come through a meat grinder as dry as hamburger.

John Shuler
St. Ignace, Michigan

Jerry's BBQ Salmon

6-8 salmon fillets
½ stick melted butter
1 T. Worcestershire sauce
1 T. lemon juice
  salt and pepper
2 T. sherry

Prepare mixture of melted butter, Worcestershire sauce, lemon juice, salt and pepper and sherry. Place fish on aluminum foil sprayed with nonstick cooking spray and put on grill. Baste salmon with liquid while cooking.

Skip Berlin
Eugene, Oregon

Joey's Favorite Salmon Bake

salmon, whole
nonstick cooking spray
seasonings to taste, such as:
  salt and pepper
  lemon juice
  parsley
  thyme
  dill
butterscotch candy disks

Fillet salmon. Lay salmon, skin-side down, on double sheet of aluminum foil sprayed with nonstick cooking spray. Season to taste. Dot every square inch with butterscotch candy disks. Bake at 450 degrees, 15 minutes for every pound of salmon

Skip Berlin
Eugene, Oregon

Latvian Salmon

> half or whole pink or red salmon
> butter
> southwestern spice (salt, spices, mesquite flavoring, jalapeno
>   powder, garlic powder, Worcestershire powder)
> lemon juice to cover fish
> 1 oz. dry sherry

Use aluminum pan with cover to snugly accommodate fish. Cover bottom of pan with butter. Sprinkle with spices. Lightly cover inside belly of fish with lemon juice. Pour dry sherry in pan, add fish, and sprinkle with more spices.

Put pan on stove and heat until wine is bubbling, then cook for 2-3 more minutes. Then turn fish over and repeat procedure. If desired, grill on charcoal grill for 1 minute on each side for added flavor.

Tal Sulmeisters
Torrington, Wyoming

Salmon Cheese Ball

> 1 lb. smoked salmon
> 8 oz. cream cheese, softened
> 2 T. horseradish
> ½ cup pecans or walnuts
> 1 T. parsley, chopped
> 1 T. chives, chopped
> 2 T. onion, minced

Mix all ingredients except nuts, parsley chives. Form into ball or log. Refrigerate, until ready to serve. Before serving, mix nuts, parsley and chives ½ hour before serving and roll ball into nut mixture just before serving.

Thomas E. Flaherty

Thomas E. Flaherty
Kewaunee, Wisconsin

Long John Soup

1 salmon carcass (preferably
    chinook, springer or silver)
1 gal. water (approximately)
3 potatoes, diced
6 carrots, sliced
1 onion, chopped
½ stalk celery, chopped
1 small can corn
½ lb. mushrooms, whole

½ gal. milk
1 stick butter
1 T. salt
    pepper
    garlic clove or garlic salt
1 can shrimp (optional)
1 can clams (optional)
1 can oysters (optional)

Put carcass in big pot and add water. Bring to boil. Reduce heat and simmer 5 minutes. Pick the bones clean and put fish back in water. Add potatoes, carrots, onions, celery, corn, mushrooms and just about anything else that makes you happy. You can also add canned shrimp, clams, or oysters for a seafood chowder.

As soup simmers, add ½ gallon milk, butter, salt, pepper and garlic. You can start cooking at medium heat for 2-3 hours. You'll have some great chowder that will make you nice and warm and sleepy while sitting in front of the fireplace in your long johns, dreaming of, well, you know what—fishing! Makes about 2 gallons, so you can freeze up a bunch while you get ready for winter.

John Evans
Portland, Oregon

Oven-Baked Fish

3-5 lb. salmon, whole
    celery salt
    salt

¼ lb. butter
1 celery stalk (about 5-6 inches long)

Prepare fish as usual. You do not need to remove skin. Salt the stomach cavity heavily with celery salt and a little table salt. Lightly salt the outer surface of the fish. Put butter into stomach cavity along with celery stalk. Wrap fish in foil, put in a flat pan, and bake at 350 degrees for 45-50 minutes.

Tom Ferguson
Brush Prairie, Washington

Poached Salmon with Dill Sauce

2 salmon fillets (8-10 oz. each)
1 cup blush or rose wine
4 cups water

1 stalk celery, diced
¼ carrot, shredded
1 lemon, sliced

Dill Sauce

3 tsp. sour cream
2 tsp. mayonnaise
   pinch granulated garlic
1 lemon wedge, for juice only
1 tsp. capers
   pinch dill weed

Poach salmon in wine and water. Bring to boil. Add celery, carrot, and sliced lemon and cook 8-10 minutes. Combine all ingredients for dill sauce and serve over poached fish.

Richard Kubel
Arroyo Grande, California

Salmon and Corn Bake

2 cups salmon, finely chopped
1 can cream-style corn
1 cup cracker crumbs
2 eggs
2 T. chopped onion
¼ tsp. salt
¼ tsp. pepper
   potato chips

Heat oven to 325 degrees. Beat eggs and mix with salmon, corn, cracker crumbs, onion, salt and pepper. Pour mixture into lightly greased 2-quart casserole. Top with crumbled potato chips. Bake about 40 minutes.

Samuel T. Gontkovsky
Dave, Florida

Salmon Ball

1 lb. salmon, flaked
8 oz. cream cheese
1 T. lemon juice
2 tsp. onion, grated
1 tsp. horseradish
1 tsp. salt
¼ tsp. liquid smoke
½ cup walnuts, chopped
3 T. parsley flakes

Combine all ingredients except nuts and parsley flakes. Mix well and shape into ball. Roll in walnuts and parsley. Chill and serve on crackers.

Clayton V. Cherney
Green Bay, Wisconsin

Salmon Balls or Patties

1 cup ground salmon, partially cooked
1 cup bread stuffing mix
1 medium onion, finely chopped
2 eggs
4 oz. medium-sharp cheddar cheese, shredded
    fish batter mix
    seasonings

Blend dry ingredients. Add eggs to hold dry ingredients together. Mix thoroughly and season to taste with your favorite seasonimgs such as, garlic salt, hickory smoked salt, white pepper, etc. Roll into balls or patties. Dip in batter and deep fry.

John Shuler
St. Ignace, Michigan

Salmon Dijonnaise

6-8 salmon fillets
¾ stick butter
2 T. lemon juice
1 T. Dijon mustard
2 T. chives or green onion, chopped.

Line pan with aluminum foil. Combine all ingredients except salmon and spread half in foil-lined pan. Lay fish on top and cover with rest of mix. Bake 10-20 minutes at 400 degrees.

Wallace Brandt
Concord, California

Salmon Flake

1 lb. salmon, cooked
¼ lb. sharp cheese
1 cup canned tomato soup
½ tsp. salt
1 tsp. mustard
1 T. Worcestershire sauce
2 eggs
1 cup evaporated milk, undiluted

Melt cheese over warm heat or in double boiler. Gradually pour in tomato soup and seasonings. Add eggs to milk and stir slowly into cheese mixture. Add salmon cooked in large pieces and heat 5-10 minutes. Serve on crisp salted crackers.

Evelyn Meuli
Wrangell, Arkansas

Salmon Loaf

- 2 cups ground salmon, partially cooked
- 1 cup bread stuffing mix
- 1 large onion, chopped
- 1 stalk celery, diced
- 2 eggs

Blend salmon, stuffing mix, onion and celery. Add eggs. Mix thoroughly. Form into loaf. Place in greased loaf pan. Bake 30-40 minutes at 350 degrees.

John Shuler
St. Ignace, Michigan

Salmon Mousse

- 6 oz. red salmon
- 1 3-oz. pkg. cream cheese
- 1 tsp. lemon juice
- 2 T. grated onion
- 1 tsp. white horseradish
- 1 tsp. parsley, chopped
  few drops liquid smoke

Allow cream cheese to come to room temperature. Flake cooked salmon. Combine all ingredients and place in a small mold. Chill. When ready to serve, turn out onto dark green curly lettuce; garnish with pimento strips and olives. Serve with crackers or cocktail bread.

David A. Brothman
Bensalem, Pennsylvania

Salmon Steaks with Yogurt Sauce

4 salmon steaks
½ cup plain yogurt
¼ cup mayonnaise-type salad dressing
¾ tsp. dillweed
½ tsp. lemon juice
⅛ tsp. pepper

Arrange steaks on broiler pan or grill. Cook 7 minutes. Turn. Cook other side 5-7 minutes or until fish flakes easily with fork. Large steaks will require more cooking time.

Meanwhile, combine remaining ingredients and blend well. Serve alongside salmon.

Terry Devine
St. Paul, Minnesota

Salmon-Stuffed Manicotti

2½ oz. smoked salmon, chopped
12 manicotti shells
1½ cups ricotta cheese
1 egg
¼ cup green onion, finely chopped

3 T. fresh dill, chopped, or 1 tsp. dried
2 T. milk
2 T. Parmesan cheese, grated
1½ cups prepared tomato sauce

Preheat oven to 350 degrees. Cook pasta in boiling water according to package directions or until firm to the bite. Drain, cover and set aside.

In bowl, combine ricotta cheese, egg, salmon, green onions, dill, milk and Parmesan cheese. Mix until smooth. Fill pasta shells. Pour half tomato sauce in bottom of 13" x 9" baking dish. Place pasta shells over sauce and pour other half tomato sauce over pasta. Cover and bake for 15-20 minutes or until hot.

Note: As an alternative to manicotti, use 24 jumbo shells. Sprinkle ¼ cup shredded mozzarella cheese over pasta shells just before serving. Can be prepared up to a day ahead with sauce poured over. Bake just before serving.

Leo G. J. Seffelaar
Broadview, Saskatchewan

Smoked Salmon Deluxe

1 lb. salmon, in chunks
1 cup brown sugar
¼ cup non-iodized salt
2 cups soy sauce
½ cup Worcestershire sauce
1 cup water
¼ cup minced onion
1 tsp. garlic powder
½ tsp. pepper
1 tsp. Tabasco sauce (optional)

Brine salmon chunks 12 or more hours in a large glass or plastic bowl (DO NOT use metal). Put a heavy plate on top to keep salmon chunks submerged in brine. Stir once or twice while brining to mix ingredients thoroughly. Keep refrigerated.

George Greiner

Dry until tacky. Place largest and thickest pieces on bottom rack of smoker. Fill chip pan with ⅔ hickory and ⅓ apple chips, using 3 pans of chips (any more are just wasted). Leave in smoker until drying is complete. This may take 12 or more hours, depending on the thickness of the meat.

Use for chinook salmon, steelhead, larger trout, and coho salmon. This is also a great recipe for beef or venison jerky.

This recipe was developed by my grandfather and has been used by four generations of the Greiner family.

George and Nancy Greiner
Jefferson, Oregon

Salmon Teriyaki

1 lb. salmon fillets
¾ cup soy sauce
¼ cup sugar
¾ cup sake (rice wine)

Cut fillets into portion-sized pieces and marinate about 30 minutes in soy sauce, sugar and sake. Remove from marinade and place under hot broiler about 4" from heat. Baste frequently with marinade. Broil about 4 minutes on each side. When nicely browned, serve, sprinkled with the warmed sauce.

For charcoal broiling, place in oiled, hinged broiler rack and broil about 7" above hot coals, basting frequently with sauce. Cook first side about 4 minutes, turn and cook other side about 6 minutes or until just nicely browned. Thickness of steaks determines time, but fish is better underdone than overdone. Serve with a little of the warmed sauce.

Note: A teriyaki coating tends to burn easily. If fish appears to be browning too fast, move farther away from flame or coals.

Bill Akira
San Gabriel, California

Okie Smoked Salmon

5 lbs. white king salmon
1 gal. water
1 lb. pickling salt
1 large pkg. brown sugar (3-4 cups)

Combine water and salt, stirring to mix well. Soak salmon in the salt mixture for 2 hours. Remove salmon, pat dry, cover, and refrigerate overnight.

Place salmon on the smoker rack with skin side down. Cover salmon liberally with brown sugar. Smoke over low heat for 6-8 hours, making sure the water pan has plenty of water throughout the cooking time. All fruit woods give a good flavor, as well as hickory and mesquite.

John M. Atkins
Blanchard, Oklahoma

Martin's Smoked Salmon

4 salmon fillets
2 qt. water
1 cup salt
1 cup brown sugar

1 tsp. garlic powder
½-1 tsp. whole pepper corns
½-1 tsp. Tabasco sauce

Warm water, salt and brown sugar until dissolved. Add garlic powder, whole pepper corns and Tabasco. Allow to cool.

Pour solution over fresh fish until covered. Leave in brine for 2 hours, then smoke for about 6 hours, depending on size of fish.

Martin Steiner
Vacaville, California

Pickled Salmon

4 salmon fillets
1 Bermuda onion, sliced
1 tsp. whole pepper corns
1 tsp. mixed pickling spice
2 cups white or cider vinegar
2 cups water
1 cup sugar

Cover salmon fillets with pickling salt and let sit overnight. In morning cut fish into cubes. Put cubes into wide-mouth jug, stopping every 2 inches. Cover with sliced Bermuda onion, 1 teaspoon whole pepper corns, 1 teaspoon mixed pickling spice. Repeat until jar is two-thirds full. Mix vinegar, water and sugar. Pour over fish, marinate in cool place for 3 days. Serve with sour cream.

Tim Oberlin

Tim Oberlin
Stryker, Ohio

Smoked Salmon Party Dip

1 cup cooked ground salmon
8 oz. cream cheese
1 medium onion, finely chopped
4 oz. medium-sharp cheddar cheese,
    shredded

favorite seasoned salt
garlic salt
liquid smoke seasoning
white pepper

Blend salmon and cream cheese thoroughly. Add onion and seasonings to taste, using season salt, garlic salt, Liquid Smoke, hickory smoked salt and white pepper. Garnish with a little paprika and parsley for color. Serve with mild crackers.

John Shuler
St. Ignace, Michigan

Steamed Whole Salmon

1 coho or king salmon, any size
1 pkg. onion soup mix
½ stick margarine, sliced lengthwise
    seasonings, such as garlic powder, salt, pepper, or your own special mix
1½ oz. white wine
3-4 oz. lemon juice

Remove innards from fish, leaving cavity clean. Head may or may not be removed. Remove scales from body. Set fish on aluminum foil and empty entire package of onion soup mix into cavity. Add margarine and seasoning. Wrap fish with foil, leaving one end open. Add white wine and lemon juice through open end. Close the second end, and wrap again with a second piece of aluminum foil. Place on heated grill for the following lengths of time.

3-5 lbs.	15 minutes each side
6-10 lbs.	25 minutes each side
10+ lbs.	30 minutes each side

Stanley E. Serlick
Libertyville, Illinois

Salmon & Steelhead Stew

This is an excellent way to use all sorts of fresh caught and store bought odds and ends. There's no real recipe so the first three sets of ingredients can depend on what's biting, or what's affordable. You can also use just one or two kinds of fish as well, and the result's a classic French stew. This hearty recipe serves eight to ten.

    3 lbs. of salmon, steelhead or other fatty fish.
    2 lbs. of uncooked crabs, cleaned or canned clams or mussels in the shell
    ½ lb. fresh shrimp or prawns in the shell
    6 T. olive oil
    2 large onions, chopped
    3 garlic cloves, minced
    1 cup of red wine (not screw top!)
    ½ cup water
    1 lb. fresh or a medium can of stewed tomatoes, chopped
    1 bay leaf
    2 T. fresh parsley
    ½ tsp. rosemary leaves
    ½ tsp. salt
    ½ tsp. pepper
    French bread

Clean and scale fish and cut into 2" thick chunks. Crack crab legs and bodies. Scrub shellfish. If your family and guests are fussy, remove the shells from the shrimp.

Heat oil in a large saucepan or Dutch oven over low heat. Note: Dutch ovens catch splatter to ease galley cleanup. Sauté onions and garlic until golden brown.

Add wine, water, tomatoes, bay leaf, parsley, rosemary and pepper. Cook ten minutes over medium heat while stirring. Add fish, crab and shellfish and cook for an additional 15 minutes or until fish flakes and shellfish opens. Discard any shells that do not open (don't cook any that weren't closed to start).

Place a one inch thick slice of French Bread in a soup bowl, divvy up the fish and shellfish and spoon on the sauce. While white wines are supposed to go with fish, we drink the same good red we use in the dish.

Lou Bignami
Moscow, Idaho

Steelhead Stuffed with Crab*

A nicely baked small salmon, steelhead or big trout stuffed with bread, crab meat and spices offers a major presentation if served surrounded by braised red potatoes or a rim of piped-on mashed potatoes. We serve it with sliced tomatoes with drizzled olive oil and basil.

3-4 lb. whole steelhead
1½ cups of ¼-inch bread cubes
  2 cups crab meat, flaked
  1 tsp. thyme leaves, dried
  1 tsp. tarragon leaves, dried
  1 T. lemon juice (at least)
  2 shallots, finely shopped
  1 egg, beaten
    salt and pepper
  2 T. butter
  1 cup white wine

Heat oven to 350 degrees. Mix bread cubes, crab, spices, lemon juice, shallots and egg. Salt and pepper to taste. Wash fish, pat dry and fill with stuffing. Place the fish, stuffing up on a buttered baking dish. Dot the top of the fish with butter and pour on wine. Note: baking fish upside down helps retain moisture

Cover fish with foil and bake 45 minutes to an hour or until the flesh along the backbone flakes. Remove from oven, invert fish back to "swimming position," pipe on potato and brush top with butter before you broil just long enough to brown the top.

* striped bass, if steamed and cooled, flakes up to exactly the taste and texture of crab body meat

Lou Bignami
Moscow, Idaho

Salmon or Steelhead Masala

Considering the length of the coast, and the number of rivers, and the fish that live in rice paddies, it's no surprise that folks eat fish in India. To start, consider a small box of Indian spices offer mild heat and exotic flavors. There are different kinds of Masala, try to find one made for fish; otherwise chicken's the choice. Sometimes you see these labeled as Tahdoori spices. The last is the name of the kind of oven traditionally used

You can, if you insist, combine coriander, chili, cumin, turmeric, black pepper, fenugreek (try the health food store) clove leaves (ditto) and garlic and onion flakes. There are all sorts of ways to bake or broil fish with this, but we're especially fond of this foil method as nothing need refrigeration.

You can cook foil wrapped fish in coals or at home in a 375 degree oven, too.

    4 salmon steaks or fillets (one per person)
    1 onion, sliced
    ¼ cup mushrooms, sliced
    4 T. of Tandoori Marsala
    4 T. of lemon juice or one lemon sliced
      Foil
      salt and pepper
      butter or oil

Heat oven to 375 degrees or prepare coals or charcoal.

Tear off four foil pieces. Note: if cooking over coals, you'll want to double wrap the fish.

Place a dab of butter on each. Rub 1 tablespoon of Marsala powder on each fish piece and put the fish on the foil. Top with other ingredients.

Note: you can dump the fish and all the seasoning in a resealable bag, shake it and carry the fish to your shore lunch. This cooks about fifteen minutes in coals and in about 30 minutes in the oven. Camp cooks may find it a bit easier and neater to put the foil packages on a rack in a Dutch oven and cover it with coals. Then open the packages and let them cook open to crisp up for about ten minutes.

We serve this right from the foil.

Lou Bignami
Moscow, Idaho

Salmon & Macaroni Casserole

Here's another good field dish that does not require refrigeration. Note: save the warm macaroni water for washing up.

2 lbs. of salmon fillets
  vegetable oil
  salt and pepper
1 onion, chopped
2 cloves garlic, minced
3 stalks of celery
1 small bell pepper
2 T. parsley, chopped
1 small can of shrimp, or ¼ lb. fresh
1 lb. of pasta (spaghetti, macaroni, etc.)
2 cans cream of mushroom soup
1 can water
½ can measure of white wine.

Fry fillets until slightly browned on both sides. Remove and set fillets in a casserole and reserve two fillets for topping. Start cooking pasta in boiling salted water to "al dente" so it still has some texture. Heat oven to 300 degrees

Sauté onion, garlic, celery, bell pepper and parsley in the "fish pan." Remove from heat and add shrimp. Mix with pasta and use the mix to cover the fish in the casserole.

Heat mushroom soup, 1 can of water and ½ can of white wine and pour over fillets. Top with two reserved fillets and bake about one hour.

Note: this works nicely in a Dutch oven.

Lou Bignami
Moscow, Idaho

Salmon & Steelhead Spread

As a summer spread for crackers, a delicious sandwich filling or even an open face sandwich topping that you can sprinkle with grated cheese and grill under the broiler, this delicious fish spread offers a wonderful treat and an exceptional way to use flaked fish of other species as well. Nice reddish-orange salmon, steelhead or trout add visual appeal.

1 cup cooked salmon, flaked
1 3-ounce package cream cheese, softened
⅓ cup sour cream
1 T. sherry
1 T. lemon juice
¼ tsp. salt
1 tsp. dillweed
  parsley garnish
  pimento for color (optional)

Mix ingredients in a small bowl and chill for two hours.

Lou Bignami
Moscow, Idaho

Poached Salmon

1½ lbs. salmon steak
4 medium carrots, unpeeled
4 stalks celery, include leaves
¼ leek
1 cup mushrooms, sliced
2 medium onions, quartered
   (including skins)
1 T. basil, fresh
2 bay leaves
1 T. dillweed, fresh
2 tsp. garlic, minced

1 tsp. parsley, fresh
½ tsp. pepper
1 tsp. salt
1 tsp. thyme, ground
8 cups water
1 T. all purpose flour
1 T. margarine
1 cup half-and-half
½ cup Parmesan cheese, grated

Add water to 6-10 quart pot. Add carrots, celery, leek, onions, basil, bay leaves, dillweed, garlic, parsley, and thyme. Bring to a boil and turn down heat to simmer. Simmer for 1 hour then remove everything from stock with slotted spoon and discard. Filter stock through fine mesh seive or cheese cloth.

Bone salmon and add to strained stock. Bring to a boil and simmer for about 5-7 minutes or until salmon is done (time varies depending on thickness of pieces). Remove salmon from pot with slotted spoon and set aside.

Make a paste with flour and margarine. Reduce stock until there is about 3 cups remaining. Add half-and-half, salt, pepper and mushrooms. Add flour paste to thicken. Add salmon and simmer just until fish is reheated.

Serve over boiled tiny red potatoes. Top fish with Parmsean cheese before serving.

Charlie Peterson
Seattle, Washington

Fried Sole

2 fresh, whole sole
½ lemon
  seasonings (your choice)
  pepper
  flour
2 T. butter
2 T. peanut oil

Wash fish under running water and scrub with lemon. Dry with paper towel.

Sprinkle with seasoning, pepper and flour. Melt butter and oil in a frying pan and let heat. Put fish in the pan and cook for about 12 minutes. Turn after the first 2 minutes and lower heat. Continue cooking, turning again after 5 minutes. Remove the sole from the pan and debone. Serve with vegetables and potato or rice.

Robert F. Kane
St. John, Nebraska

Buttery Poor Man's Lobster

  sturgeon
  butter
  salt and pepper
  lemon

Cut sturgeon into 1" cubes. Bring pan of water to boil. Toss in fish. Boil for 2 minutes. Drain. Serve with salt, pepper, lemon and melted butter mixed together for dipping.

Jack Kelly
Black Diamond, Washington

Three-Cheese Sturgeon

1 sturgeon fillet
3 T. butter
  salt, pepper and garlic powder
3 cheeses, your choice, grated

Place sturgeon in shallow glass baking dish. Add salt, pepper and garlic powder to taste. Dot with butter. Cover with foil and bake until fish is flaky. Drain off excess juice. Sprinkle cheeses over fillet. Heat just until cheese melts. Serve hot.

Susan Ostenberg
Black Diamond, Washington

Baked Trout in Foil

4 trout, 12-14 inches (cleaned)
7 green onions, finely chopped
2 celery stalks, finely chopped
3 carrots, medium-sized, finely chopped
⅓ cup margarine
8 lemon wedges
  salt and pepper

Saute vegetables in margarine until soft.

Rub each trout with butter or margarine and place on a sheet of foil that has been oiled or buttered. Put vegetable mixture in cavity of each fish, using equal amounts per fish. Place each foil package open on a cookie sheet. Place under broiler until skin is brown (about 5 minutes). Remove from broiler.

Close each individual foil package. Put on cookie sheet in oven at 425 degrees and bake for 15-20 minutes.

Using spatula, remove the trout to a heated platter. Serve immediately with lemon wedges.

John Campbell
Blairsville, Pennsylvania

Frank Cavaliere

Italian Trout

1 12-14 inch trout
½ medium yellow onion, sliced
½ bell pepper, sliced
1 16-oz. can crushed tomatoes
1 T. crushed red pepper
1 T. Italian seasoning
2 cloves fresh garlic, crushed

Place trout in casserole dish. Add remaining ingredients and bake at 400 degrees for 15-20 minutes or until fish flakes easily.

Frank Cavaliere
Farmington, New Mexico

Classic Pecan Trout

6 trout fillets, 7-9 oz. each, thawed
2-3 lemons for juice
1½ cups pecans, very finely chopped
    salt and pepper to taste
4 T. margarine or butter

Marinate trout in fresh lemon juice overnight. In a heavy skillet, melt butter or margarine. Remove fillets from marinade and salt and pepper to taste. Coat the seasoned fillets with the chopped pecans and cook in the hot butter for 10-15 minutes, turning once.

Elvin Sample
Cassville, Missouri

Bar B Q'd Long Island Connetquot Trout

1 trout, 2-3 lbs.
2 carrots
3 stalks celery
1 red or green bell pepper
1 onion
1 tomato
¼ cup lemon herb salad dressing

1 T. dill weed
1 tsp. garlic powder
1 tsp. ground ginger
    salt and pepper
    cilantro or capers (optional)

Slice carrots, celery, pepper, onion and tomato into chunks. Put in large mixing bowl. Coat with herb dressing. Add dillweed, garlic powder, ginger and salt and pepper to taste.

Clean trout, leaving head, tail and skin on. Fill trout cavity with vegetable mixture. Place on large sheet of foil. Surround trout with remaining mixture. Wrap tight with foil, using extra if needed. Put on grill and flip every 5 minutes for 20-30 minutes, depending on size of trout. When foil is opened, skin will stick to it. Enjoy with baked potato and a nice wine.

Vincent Balzano
Seaford, New York

Broiled Trout

1 fresh trout, gutted
½ stick butter
1 tsp. lemon and pepper seasoning salt
¼ tsp. garlic salt
¼ tsp. onion powder
⅛ tsp. poultry seasoning

Stuff trout with ¼ stick of butter. Melt rest of butter and add lemon pepper, garlic salt, onion powder, and poultry seasoning. Spread ½ mixture on trout.

Broil 7-10 minutes. Flip trout and spread remaining mixture over fish. Broil 3-5 minutes longer

Tim Mattison
Hayfield, Minnesota

Butterfly Fillets with Island Sauce

1 rainbow trout, 12-14 oz., filleted
2 cups chicken stock
½ tsp. thyme
1 T. onion, minced
½ tsp. nutmeg
4 tsp. flour
1 cup heavy cream
1 cup melted butter
1 tsp. lemon juice
½ tsp. salt
¼ tsp. pepper
2 T. butter or margarine
parsley

Combine chicken stock, thyme, onion and nutmeg in a saucepan and bring to a boil. Reduce heat and simmer until mixture is reduced to 2-3 tablespoons. Add flour to make a roux and cook for 1 minute. Add cream, stirring constantly until smooth. Heat until sauce thickens. Add butter, lemon juice and seasonings.

Place fillets on a greased barbecue rack and brush with melted butter or margarine. Grill 4-5 minutes on each side, basting occasionally. Serve trout on individual plates with sauce. Garnish with parsley.

Ronald F. Kane
St. John, Nebraska

Trout on the Grill

1 trout
½ cup almonds, slivered
3-4 orange slices

3-4 lemon slices
margarine

Put almonds and orange slices inside trout. Put lemon slices on top. Salt and pepper inside and brush outside with margarine. Wrap in foil and put on grill for 7 minutes on each side.

Ruth Ann Donley
Mount Joy, Pennsylvania

Fennel Stuffing for Trout

1 trout per person
1½ T. shallots, chopped
1½ T. parsley, chopped
4 T. clarified butter
½ cup fine white bread crumbs
1 egg

¼ tsp. dried fennel
salt and pepper
4 T. fresh butter
1 T. chopped parsley
juice of ½ lemon

Cook shallots and parsley in 1 tablespoon hot clarified butter over low heat for 2 minutes. Add bread crumbs and stir well. Add unbeaten egg and fennel. Stir constantly until the mixture thickens. Remove from heat and season to taste.

Cut gills off of trout with scissors. Cut backbone from within the belly just behind the head and in front of tail and remove. Sprinkle the inside with salt and pepper. Fill with stuffing and press closed.

Preheat oven to 350 degrees. Heat remainer of clarified butter in a large oven-proof skillet or pan. Put in the trout and cook over medium heat. Turn trout over and put the pan in the oven. Cook 15-18 minutes, according to the size of the trout. Season with salt and pepper. When trout is cooked, transfer to a heated platter. Pour off all fat from the pan and add fresh butter. Add chopped parsley and let the butter melt over low heat. Add juice of ½ lemon. Pour pan butter over trout and serve immediately.

Bill Akira
San Gabriel, California

Grilled Trout with Garlic and Rosemary

4 trout, pan dressed
2 tsp. olive oil
4 cloves garlic, minced or pressed
4 sprigs fresh rosemary
1 lemon, quartered

Preheat charcoal grill. Rinse trout inside and out; pat dry. Rub olive oil and garlic inside and out of each trout and put one sprig of rosemary in each. Cook over medium heat until opaque through the thickest part, 3-4 minutes on each side. Serve with lemon wedges alongside for squeezing.

Manual Silva, Jr.
San Jose, California

Herb-Baked Trout

4 trout, cleaned
 vegetable oil
 lemon juice, fresh
 salt and pepper
4 T. each of chopped parsley, chives, dill
4 T. butter or margarine.

You need 4 pieces of aluminum foil large enough to completely enclose each trout. Rub trout lightly with oil and lemon juice. Place trout on foil and sprinkle with salt and pepper. Sprinkle each with 1 tablespoon parsley, chives and dill. Top each with 1 tablespoon butter. Fold foil, making sure it is sealed. Bake at 375 degrees for 25 minutes or until fish flakes when tested with fork. Transfer to plates carefully. Serve hot.

Bryan Lasher
Union City, Pennsylvania

Irish-Baked Trout

4 cleaned whole trout, about 8 oz. each
  salt
4 green onions, sliced
1 green pepper, chopped
¼ cup margarine
1 cup soft bread crumbs
¼ cup snipped parsley
1 tsp. lemon juice
1 tsp. salt
¼ tsp. dried basil leaves

Cook and stir onions and peppers in margarine until onions are tender. Remove from heat. Stir in bread crumbs, parsley, lemon juice, salt and basil. Rub cavities of each fish with salt, then staff each with about ¼ cup stuffing mixture. Place fish in greased rectangular baking dish, 13" x 9" x 2". Bake uncovered at 350 degrees until fish flakes easily with fork, 30-35 minutes. Serve hot.

Bryan Lasher
Union City, Pennsylvania

Lake Trout Special

3-5 lb. lake trout
  garlic salt
  lemon pepper
  onion flakes
  butter-flavored salt
  mayonnaise
  lemon

Clean and skin trout, removing head and fins. Coat entire fish, inside and out, with mayonnaise. Sprinkle lemon pepper, onion flakes and flavored salt lightly over fish, inside and out. Slice half the lemon and put it in body cavity. Wrap in foil and bake at 350 degrees for 12-13 minutes per pound.

Leon Dusseau
Moravia, New York

Microwaved Trout

4 medium trout
12 saltine crackers, crushed
    onion salt
    garlic powder
    Italian seasoning
    butter

Wash trout under cold running water, being sure to clean blood from belly section. Cut off tail and pat dry. Crush saltine crackers well and mix with onion salt, garlic powder, and Italian seasoning.

Apply butter to the inside of the trout and to outer skin. Roll buttered trout in seasoned cracker mixture and place, belly up, on a microwave dish. Cover with a paper towel and cook on high for 4 minutes. Remove from microwave and broil in range for 2 minutes.

John M. Atkins
Blanchard, Oklahoma

Fresh Pan-Fried Lakers

    fresh lake trout fillets
    favorite beer
    cooking oil
    breading or cracker crumbs

Soak fish in beer for 1-2 hours. Heat pan with about ¼" cooking oil to 400 degrees. Drain fillets and bread with favorite breading. Fry to golden brown, about 3 minutes on each side. Serve hot.

Ed Eichten
Center City, Minnesota

Ed Eichten

Stuffed Lake Trout

4-5 lbs. dressed trout
⅔ cup butter
¾ cup celery, finely chopped
¼ cup onion, finely chopped
2 tsp. parsley, finely chopped
3 cups Ritz crackers, crumbled
¼ cup hot water
½ lb. shrimp, cooked and diced
½ tsp. salt
¼ tsp. pepper
½ tsp. rosemary
   bacon slices

Melt butter, add vegetables, and saute until tender. Mix water with crackers, then add crackers to vegetables. Mix in shrimp, salt, pepper and rosemary. Mix again.

Clean and wash fish and dry with absorbent paper towels. Sprinkle with

Barbara Stoudnour

salt, inside and out. Stuff fish loosely with vegetable and cracker mixture and sew the opening shut with string or close with skewers. Lay slices of bacon over top of each fish.

Bake at 350 degrees for 40-60 minutes or until fish flakes. Baste occasionally with drippings. Serve immediately. Makes 8 servings.

Barbara Stoudnour
Forked River, New Jersey

130

Pan Fried Brook Trout

4 brook trout, cleaned, with head and tail left on
2 T. flour
  salt
7 T. butter
3 T. oil
2 T. lemon juice
2 T. minced chives

Rinse fish under cold running water and pat dry with paper towels. Dust lightly with flour and sprinkle with salt. In a large skillet, melt 3 tablespoons butter and oil. When it is hot, put in the trout and fry over medium-high heat until browned. Turn and brown the other side. Each side will take about 3 minutes. Melt the remaining butter with lemon juice and chives in a small saucepan. When the trout is done, transfer to a warm platter and pour sauce over trout.

Cheryl Birch
Lublin, Wisconsin

Smoked Rainbow Trout

3-4 trout, cleaned
  1 cup coarse light-brown sugar
  ½ cup coarse pickling salt
  ¼ tsp. each of oregano, ground cardamom, garlic powder, tarragon, ground
      bay leaves, ground cumin seeds and black pepper

Combine dry ingredients and rub mixture into flesh side of rainbow trout that have been split with back bone removed. Place in refrigerator for 12-24 hours in plastic container (not metal). Remove and rinse fish in cold water. Air dry until tacky. Smoke in cold smoke (under 150 degrees) for 12-24 hours or until desired texture of color and dryness.

Martin C. Carver
Surrey, British Columbia

Stuffed Trout

  1 5-lb. trout
  ¼ cup margarine
  2 cloves garlic
  ½ onion, chopped
  ½ tsp. Lawry's Seasoning Salt
  2 stalks celery, chopped in ¼-inch pieces
  1 red or green bell pepper, chopped
  1 cup peas
  2 cups carrots, chopped in ¼-inch pieces
  1 cup cucumber
  1 cup zucchini or other squash

Mix all ingredients except fish in a large saucepan or Dutch oven and warm 5-10 minutes over medium heat. Save the liquid.

  2 lemons, sliced ¼-inch thick
  ¼ cup unsalted butter
  ½ cup extra dry vermouth
  ½ tsp. salt
  1 T. lemon juice

Grease 2" deep baking pan large enough for fish. Put fish on lemon slices. Salt inner cavity. Stuff vegetables into cavity. Use extra around tail section to increase tail area to about the same size as body of fish. Put lemon slices and sliced butter on top and sides of fish. Mix lemon juice, vermouth and vegetable liquid and pour over fish. Cover pan with aluminum foil and bake at 350 degrees 1 hour. Baste every 15 minutes.

Kenneth S. Eaton, Jr.
June Lake, California

Stuffed Rainbow Trout

4 boneless rainbow trout
½ lb. cooked flaked fish, baby
    shrimp, crab meat or any
    combination
½ cup bread crumbs
½ cup croutons
¼ cup green onion, chopped
¼ cup celery, chopped
2 T. butter, melted

½ tsp. sage
⅛ tsp. pepper
½ tsp. salt
¼ tsp. marjoram
¼ tsp. garlic
1 egg, beaten
½ cup white wine
¼ cup butter, melted (reserved)

Combine all ingredients (except reserved butter) and moisten with wine. Divide stuffing into 4 parts and press lightly into the belly of each trout. Place fish on their sides on greased baking dish. Brush with reserved butter. Bake at 425 degrees for 20-25 minutes.

Laurie and Lynda MacIntosh
Winnipeg, Manitoba

Trout á la Salsa

1 trout, whole, cleaned
1 16-oz. jar of your favorite salsa
3-4 whole cloves garlic, crushed
    salt and pepper

In bowl, combine salsa and crushed garlic. Stir well. Salt and pepper the fish well, inside and out. Place a piece of heavy-duty foil (large enough to make a pouch) on cookie sheet. Spread a layer of salsa on foil, roughly the same length and width as the fish. Put fish on top of salsa. Fill the body cavity with salsa, and spread salsa over the top of the fish. Make a tight pouch. Bake at 350 degrees for 25 minutes. When fish is cooked, place pouch on platter. Roll back foil to form wall around fish so juices won't be lost. Scrape skin and salsa off fish and push aside. Liquid created in the cooking process is great for dipping.

Lou Marconnot
Woburn, Massachusetts

Trout Baked in Cream

    4 whole rainbow trout (1-2 lbs. each), cleaned
    2 T. fresh lemon juice
    1 tsp. dill weed
    1 tsp. salt
    ¼ tsp. pepper
    1 pt. whipping cream
    2 T. dry bread crumbs, finely ground

Wash and pat fish dry. Brush inside and out with lemon juice and sprinkle with dill weed and salt and pepper. Place in a lightly buttered baking dish. Pour cream over fish. Sprinkle with bread crumbs. Bake at 400 degrees for 15 minutes or until fish flakes when probed with a fork. Serve with oven-roasted potatoes.

Bryan Lasher
Union City, Pennsylvania

Trout Italiano

    4 trout fillets, skinless
    1 jar tomato sauce
    6 oz. mozzarella cheese, shredded
    2 oz. Parmesan cheese, freshly shredded
      salt to taste

Spread tomato sauce over bottom of a baking dish. Arrange fish in a single layer over the sauce. Sprinkle salt and cheeses over fish. Bake in a 400-degree oven about 20 minutes or until fish flakes.

Gene R. Harper
Memphis, Tennessee

Trout on the Grill

4 trout whole, cleaned
1 stick butter
4 green onions, chopped
3 lemons
    salt and pepper to taste

Melt butter in saucepan. Add chopped onion and juice of 1 lemon. Thinly slice another lemon and place slices in cavities of each trout. Salt and pepper each trout inside and out. Brush on butter mixture, spooning onions into cavity of each trout. Grill over hot coals for about 6 minutes on each side. Brush with leftover butter while cooking. Serve with lemon wedges.

David A. Walker
St. Louis, Missouri

Trout on the Trail

2 trout, whole, cleaned
1 pt. wild raspberries, freshly picked

Stuff cavity of cleaned fish with berries. Wrap in aluminum foil and put on coals of campfire for 30 minutes to 1 hour, depending on the size of the fish. Remove carefully and be careful of steam when foil is rolled back. Enjoy with baked potato and beer.

Tom Swords
Trenton, New Jersey

Ted's Secret Fish Dish

6 trout fillets (1 lb. each)
2 cups mayonnaise
¼ cup soy sauce
   garlic powder to taste
   seasoning salt to taste
1 bunch fresh green onions,
   chopped
1 lb. fresh mushrooms
2 lemons
   salt and pepper to taste

Michael David

Build a pan out of aluminum foil large enough to accommodate fillets. Place pan on cookie sheet. Lay fillets in foil.

In a bowl, combine soy sauce and mayonnaise until mixture is light brown. Squeeze lemon juice on fillets and rub into fish. Sprinkle with seasonings as desired. Generously cover fillets with mayo-soy mixture. Top with chopped fresh green onions and sliced mushrooms.

Carefully slide foil pan from cookie sheet onto a preheated BBQ grill. Cook at medium heat until fillets become flaky and meat pulls away from skin easily with a fork. Fish is easily separated from skin with a spatula. No extra sauce needed.

Note: This, my favorite Idaho trout recipe, also happens to be my brother Ted's favorite Washington king salmon recipe. In fact, although I'd just love to claim it, any credit should go to my big brother. Not only does he deserve it, he demands it! I spent the better part of one summer begging for this recipe and a very long, long-distance phone call begging for permission to print it for NAFC Members. There is, however, a very good reason why my brother hesitates to release this secret; you need only try it once to be hooked on its uniqueness! Our debate on species of fish to prepare will continue, but in my honest opinion, this recipe would be outstanding for any fish you could land!

Michael David
Idaho Falls, Idaho

Trout with Salsa

4 trout fillets
½ cup fresh lemon or grapefruit juice
2 T. extra-virgin olive oil

Marinate fish in lemon/grapefruit juice and olive oil for at least 1 hour.

Cut the following vegetables in big chunks, brush with olive oil and grill until browned:

1 small eggplant or zucchini
1 green pepper, seeded

1 red pepper, seeded
6 green onions or 2-3 leeks

For salsa, mix together:

½ cup black olives, chopped
1 cup black beans, drained and chopped
1 can chili peppers, drained and chopped
2-3 T. fresh grapefruit juice
2 T. olive oil
   salt and pepper to taste

Salsa can be spiced up with lemon rind, japapenos and any citrus juice.

Grill trout 2-3 minutes on each side. Serve at once with grilled vegetables and salsa.

Betty Werner
Rantoul, Illinois

Lemon Trout

2 trout fillets, average size
   lemon
   butter

Squeeze lemon juice on fillets and let sit until most of juice is absorbed. Put some butter in pan and let melt over medium heat. Put fillets in pan and cook until brown. Remove from pan and serve with lemon wedges.

Tim Bardwell
Scotia, New York

Trout with Shrimp Stuffing

3-4 trout, 8-12 inches
1 large onion
1 green pepper
1 stalk celery
6 oz. fresh mushrooms
¼ lb. butter
½ T. thyme
½ T. garlic powder
1 T. parsley flakes
  salt and pepper to taste
1 6½ oz. can broken shrimp, drained and rinsed
1 egg
⅓ cup milk
3 cups bread cubes
1 8-oz. can tomato sauce
4 T. Parmesan cheese

Dice ½ onion and green pepper, the entire stalk of celery, and about 2 ounces of the mushrooms. Slice the remaining onion, pepper and mushrooms and set aside. Saute diced onion, pepper, celery, and mushrooms in butter about 15 minutes. Add spices and shrimp. Set aside.

In mixing bowl, beat milk and egg together. Stir in bread cubes. Then stir in the shrimp mixture. Mix remaining sliced vegetables together and place in bottom of baking dish.

Stuff trout with shrimp mixture and place with any remaining stuffing over vegetables. Cover evenly with tomato sauce and sprinkle with Parmesan cheese. Cover and bake at 350 degrees for 1 hour.

Ronald Sikowski
Crivitz, Wisconsin

Baked Trout

2 lbs. trout, whole or filleted
½ tsp. garlic, minced
   salt and freshly ground black pepper
¼ cup extra virgin olive oil
   mixture of fresh herbs including parsley, basil, tarragon,
      oregano, rosemary and marjoram
1 lemon, sliced

Place the trout or fillets on a large piece of aluminum foil. Brush the foil with some olive oil. Season it with some salt and black pepper. Finely chop the herbs with the garlic to make a herb/garlic pesto and sprinkle over the trout to cover completely. Or, if using whole trout, stuff into the cavity. Lay a few thin slices of lemon over the top and wrap the foil tightly. Place in a baking dish and bake in the oven at 350 degrees until done (it could take around 20 minutes or so on average). When cooked, remove from the foil, remove the lemon slices and drizzle some more olive oil over the top if you wish and serve with wedges of lemon.

Steve Erickson
Duluth, Minnesota

Broiled Lake Trout

1 large lake trout
   butter or margarine
½ tsp. garlic, minced
   fresh parsley
2 T. olive oil
¼ tsp. white pepper, ground

Preheat the broiler. Bone the fish and flatten it out. Rub a small saucer generously with minced garlic. Mix the olive oil and white pepper in the saucer. Rub this mixture on both sides of the fish. Place the fish on a greased shallow pan. Broil until brown, turning once. Spread with butter or margarine. Garnish with parsley. Serve hot.

Jerry Nelson
Fargo, North Dakota

Tiny Trout with Burned-in Herbs

The best eating trout of all may be small brook trout from cold streams; the worst are stubby-fin rainbows off hatchery trucks. Eat the former, smoke the latter and turn them into fish pate' or give them to friends you don't like that much.

Since brook trout tend to overpopulate and stunt where limited fishing pressure permits, you can catch a bag full of eight or nine inch trout that might be two or three inches of head. So there's no need to feel guilty about keeping these fish.

This recipe fries the trout in a thick batter and then tops it off with an unusual garlic sauce. It's a dandy with lake smelt, herring and other "little bitty" fish like bluegills too. Add enough garlic and even "truck trout" taste good.

2 lbs. of small trout, cleaned
1 cup flour
3-6 T. cold water
    salt
    frying oil

Sauce:

4 slices bread crusts trimmed off
    soaked in water for 10 minutes
4-6 cloves garlic, chopped
2 T. lemon juice

4-5 T. olive oil
    salt and pepper
    parsley for garnish

Heat oil to about 375 degrees.

Mix flour, salt and a little water into a thick batter (pancake mix works too).

Dip fish into the batter ,and then cook them one or two at a time into oil until they turn golden. Caution: too many fish at once cool oil and make a greasy result.

Chop up the bread and garlic in a food processor. Add lemon juice. Keep blender or processor running and drizzle in oil in a thin stream. Check consistency. You may have to add a little water if the sauce is too thick. It should be about like maple syrup at room temperature. Then put fish on warm dishes and cover with sauce.

Lou Bignami
Moscow, Idaho

Cold Trout & Almond Soup

If you want something cool for summer days when it's so hot the mosquitoes hide, this Spanish dish is the way to go. We picked this up from a California almond grower on a day when it topped 110 degrees.

½ lb. cooked trout in small chunks
½ lb. uncooked almonds
4 cups boiling water
1 lb. white bread
1 qt. cold water
2 cloves garlic, finely minced
1 cup extra virgin olive oil
½ cup white wine or rice wine vinegar
  salt and pepper

Cover the almonds with boiling water and soak for an hour.

Cut crusts from the bread and break bread up. Cover with a quart of cold water. Then drain the almonds and put them into a blender with the garlic. Blend until smooth. Add eggs and continue to blend. Then, as the blender whirs away pour the oil in a little bit at a time.

Squeeze the bread dry, add the bread to the blender and continue to blend as you add the vinegar, salt and pepper.

Pour the soup into a cold bowl. Beat in water a bit at a time until you get the consistency you like best. Then barely stir in the trout so the pieces stay whole. Cool at least four hours - this soup can be made ahead! Then serve.

If you like you can garnish the soup with whatever is handy. Salted, roasted almonds look nice as a topping and add texture. So do grapes–both green and red offer a nice color contrast. We've added sprigs of mint as well.

Lou Bignami
Moscow, Idaho

Rosemary Trout with Ham or Prosciutto

I don't like "truck trout" as the rather tasteless flesh seems to stick to the bones. This preparation avoids that by boning out the trout, and enough ham and butter make most things edible. A small, sharp knife lets you slice off the ribs and remove the backbone and head. If you chicken out with a boning knife you can always go to flatter fish, like panfish.

4 trout, boned
1 oz. of ham or prosciutto cut in strips or cubes
   fresh rosemary
4 pats of butter
   flour
   paprika
   white wine that you'd drink for dinner

Heat oven to 350 degrees.

Put half the ham or prosciutto and the rosemary into the trout where you've removed its backbone without cutting through the skin. If you blow it, don't worry, serve both sides separately and don't tell your guests.

Place the trout in a buttered baking dish or heavy iron pan. Top the trout with a pat of butter small amount of flour and paprika; if you mind the fish curling as it cooks, use something like a small tin to keep the trout flat.

Cook about 10 minutes. Baste with juice from pan and top with remaining meat. Brown under broiler and serve. Delicate new potatoes, peas and a salad complete this meal nicely.

Lou Bignami
Moscow, Idaho

Trout with Herbs ("Truite Meuniere aux Herbes")

Okay, this or it's sister dish "aux fine herbes" are so classic they are standards at the type of pretentious restaurants that include French on the menus and a swarmy waiter named "Ralph" who's "yours for the night." But this dish is seldom done correctly because, like Swiss "blue trout", it requires a very fresh fish with decent texture. So you can do it better at home.

The dish, reportedly started when a miller "le meunier" caught a trout out of the millrace so the fish was cleaned, dredged in flour and fried. Then the miller's wife tossed butter and herbs into the pan, deglazes the pan with a little lemon juice and served the result hot and sizzling. The keys to perfection here are a fresh wild trout just out of the water, a hot pan, fresh herbs and cooking trout one or two at a time so they're perfectly done.

4 medium-sized trout	2 T. of fresh herbs—parsley, shallot greens,
flour	chervil, dill, tarragon or thyme
salt and pepper	lemon slices for garnish
½ stick butter	
juice of a lemon	

Dredge trout with flour, season with salt and pepper. Melt half the butter in a large hot pan so trout browns evenly, cook two fish, head to tail, at a time. 5-10 minutes a side works for 8-15" trout, respectively. Keep the dorsal side of the trout to the center of the pan (it's usually hotter and you get a more even result).

Tip: leave the dorsal fin in and when you think the fish is done wiggle the fin. If it pulls out easily the trout is done. This works with most fish.

Remove trout from pan and immediately add the other half of the butter. Cook just until butter starts to brown, then add herbs and lemon juice. When butter sizzles, pour it over the trout.

We serve this with a good white wine, saffron rice and a salad and add a lethally rich desert.

Lou Bignami
Moscow, Idaho

Twice-Baked Tuna

1 tuna, cleaned
3 T. lemon juice
3 T. margarine, melted

Grease a large baking pan, 2" high. Remove all fins, head and tail from fish. Flour all over, including fin cavities and stomach cavity. Bake at 350 degrees until fish will separate from the bone. Place both halves, head to tail, flesh side up. Remove all rib bones with a fork.

While fish is baking, make the following sauce:

2 8-oz. cans crushed tomatoes
1 16-oz. can tomato sauce
2 T. cider vinegar
2 T. Worcestershire sauce
   salt and pepper
1 tsp. chili powder
¼ tsp. Tabasco sauce
1 tsp. red paprika

Mix sauce ingredients and bring to a boil. Sprinkle the fish with lemon juice, then with melted margarine. Ladle hot sauce over the fish until the sauce is gone. Return to oven again and bake until sauce is bubbling all over. Serve hot.

Milton W. Jewell
W. Keansburg, New Jersey

Baked Walleye

    1 lb. walleye fillets
    1 cup orange juice
    ½ tsp. salt
    ¼ tsp. pepper
    ½ tsp. dry mustard
    2 pkgs. powdered chicken bouillon

Place fish fillets in a bowl with orange juice and refrigerate. Allow to marinate for 1-2 hours.

Preheat oven to 350 degrees. Combine all dry ingredients in a small bowl or paper bag. Add fillets one at a time and coat well. Bake in a shallow dish for 15-20 minutes or until fish flakes apart easily with a fork.

Dale Jenkins
Shelby, Ohio

Max's Walleye

    4 walleye fillets
    1 egg
    ½ cup milk
        instant potato flakes
        Cajun seasonings

Mix egg with milk. Mix instant potato flakes and Cajan seasoning well. Dip fillets in milk and egg batter, then dredge fillets in potato flake mixture. Fry on both sides until golden brown.

Max R. Reiss
York, Pennsylvania

Max R. Reiss

Jack Houston

Old-Fashioned Walleye

4 walleye or sauger fillets
2 eggs
½ cup lemon-lime soda
2 cups Italian seasoned
   bread crumbs

2 tsp. garlic salt
½ tsp. pepper
1½ T. onion, very finely chopped
1 lemon
   vegetable oil

Mix eggs and soda in medium-sized bowl. Let sit while mixing other ingredients.

Combine bread crumbs, garlic salt, pepper and chopped onion in a plastic bag. Mix well, being careful to coat onion thoroughly.

In large frying pan or electric skillet, add ¼" vegetable oil and heat to 350-375 degrees. Put fillets in egg and soda mixture, cover thoroughly, and let set for 5 minutes. Pour bread crumb mixture on a large dinner plate, lay fillets in crumbs, one at a time, covering completely. Shake off excess and lay fish in skillet. Do not overcook, as fillets will harden. Turn when golden brown. Remove from skillet, allowing oil to drip off. Put on platter. Garnish with ¼ lemon wedge on each filet to be squeezed if desired. These taste great with honey cornbread, steam-fried potatoes with onion and home-grown sliced tomatoes.

Jack Houston
Quincy, Illinois

Fish Toast

½ lb. walleye, cooked, skinned
    and chopped
2 strips bacon, finely chopped
4 water chestnuts, finely chopped
1 large green onion with top,
    finely chopped
2 T. all-purpose flour

1 tsp. cornstarch
1 tsp. salt
¼ tsp. ginger root, finely chopped
¼ tsp. white or ⅛ tsp. black pepper
¼ tsp. sesame oil
    vegetable oil
7 slices of white bread

Heat 1 cup of water to boiling. Add bacon and heat to boiling again. Cover and boil for 2 minutes. Drain.

Mix bacon, fish, water chestnuts, ¼ cup water, green onion, flour, cornstarch, salt, pepper, gingerroot and sesame oil.

Heat vegetable oil in a skillet. Remove crust from bread and cut each slice into 4 squares. Spread 1 teaspoon fish mixture over each square. Fry squares until golden brown, turning frequently (about 2½ minutes). Drain on paper towels.

Bryan Lasher
Union City, Pennsylvania

Broiled Walleye

1 lb. walleye fillets
¼ cup butter
    salt and pepper to taste
2 T. lime juice
¼ cup mayonnaise
¼ cup Ritz cracker crumbs

Brown butter in a skillet and set aside. Put fillets in a baking dish and sprinkle with salt, pepper and lime juice. Spread mayonnaise over fillets. Sprinkle fillets with cracker crumbs. Pour brown butter over fillets. Cook under broiler until fish flakes when tested with a fork.

F. A. (Fritz) Backscheider
Batavia, Ohio

Fritz's Walleye

4-6 walleye fillets
    salt and pepper
2 T. lemon juice
2 tomatoes, sliced
1 green pepper, sliced thin
1 Bermuda onion, sliced
½ cup Italian dressing

Line baking dish with fillets. Add salt, pepper and lemon juice. Cover fillets with tomatoes, green peppers, and Bermuda onions. Pour Italian dressing over all and bake at 350 degrees for 40 minutes

F. A. (Fritz) Backscheider
Batavia, Ohio

Melt-in-Your-Mouth Walleye

6-8 walleye fillets
½ lb. butter (more if necessary, depending on amount of fish)
3 cups cracker meal or crushed saltine crackers
2 cups milk
1 egg, beaten

Place cracker crumbs in a large shallow bowl. Pat fillets dry with paper towels. Melt butter in large skillet over low to medium heat. Put milk and beaten egg in two separate bowls.

Dip fillets into milk, then into egg, then coat each side with cracker meal. Place in skillet. Cook until lightly browned on each side. Don't overcook. Flesh should flake when tested with fork. Serve hot.

Howard T. Martin
Eau Claire, Wisconsin

Mmm, Mmm Good Walleye

    1 lb. walleye fillets
    ½ stick butter
    3 T. green pepper, diced
    3 T. onion, diced
    ¼ tsp. black pepper
    ¼ tsp. garlic salt

Double wrap everything in foil. Place on grill at medium to high heat. Close lid and check occasionally. Grill 20-30 minutes or until fish flakes and onion and peppers are tender.

Judy Cope
Oil City, Pennsylvania

Steamed Fish Shore Lunch

4-5 walleyes, filleted
    1 can stewed tomatoes
    1 onion, sliced
    1 lemon, sliced
      salt
      pepper
      oregano
      butter or margarine

Arrange half of fillets on a large piece of buttered aluminum foil. Drain juice from can of stewed tomatoes. Spread half the stewed tomatoes over fish. Spread slices of onion and lemon over fillets. Sprinkle with salt, pepper and oregano. Arrange second layer of fillets and repeat all ingredients on top of fillets.

Press second sheet of aluminum foil on top and securely roll all edges several times to assure no leaks. Place on grate over low charcoal fire or glowing coals of campfire until foil "puffs" up full of steam. Poke 4-5 holes in top layer of foil to allow steam to escape. Continue cooking about 10 minutes longer. Remove from heat and serve with boiled new potatoes with butter and lemon juice drizzled on top and coleslaw.

Gerald E. Wixson
Lee's Summit, Missouri

Walleye Italiano

6-8 walleye fillets
3 cups flour
2 envelopes tomato soup mix
2 pkgs. Italian dressing mix
1 tsp. salt
1 T. paprika
¼ lb. butter or margarine

Combine all dry ingredient in a heavy resealable plastic bag. Shake well. Prepare a baking pan or cookie sheet with nonstick cooking spray or wipe it well with cooking oil. Coat fillets by placing in bag of seasoned flour and shaking. Make sure both sides of the fillet are coated. Arrange coated fillets on the prepared pan.

Melt ¼ pound butter or margarine and drizzle over the exposed surface of each fillet divided equally on all fillets. Bake uncovered without turning at 375 degrees for 20-30 minutes or until golden brown. Test with fork to ensure flesh is flaky. Don't overcook. Also excellent with crappie, bluegill, bass or northern pike.

Howard T. Martin
Eau Claire, Wisconsin

Walleye Pike á là Norma

6 walleye fillets
2 eggs, beaten
1 cup Ritz crackers, crushed
½ stick butter, melted

Dip fillets in egg. Roll in crushed crackers. Lay fillets on aluminum foil on cookie sheet. Drip butter over fillets. Bake 15 minutes at 350-400 degrees.

Norma Ostrom
Minneapolis, Minnesota

Norma Ostrom

Nutty Walleye Fillets

Walleye are so good to eat that simple preparations often seem to work best unless you catch and keep a lot of fish. Fresh walleye fillets are perfect, and fillets frozen in water hold up for six months.

Do eviserate your filleted fish and save backbones, heads and such for the stock pot that produces both stock for sauces and a surprising amount of walleye flakes for chowder, fish cakes and the like. Then too, experts know that walleye cheeks, like salmon cheeks, are the sweetest of all. You can prepare cheeks exactly like the following fillet recipe.

- 2 lbs. of walleye fillets
- 6 T. butter
  salt and pepper
- ¼ cup milk
- ¼ cup flour
- 2 T. nut pieces (pecans, almonds, walnuts, hazelnuts or macademia nuts, as you like)
- 2 tsp. lemon juice

Melt four tablespoons of butter in a heavy skillet over medium heat. Do adjust heat so butter gets golden, but not black! If you burn the butter claim "blackened walleye" intentions, or start over!

Pat fillets dry. Season with salt and pepper, dip in milk and then in flour. Cook fillets in a heavy pan on both sides – 10 minutes per inch of thickness total – or until the thickest section of the fillet flakes with a fork.

Remove fish to a warm serving dish or dinner plate.

Immediately add remaining butter and nuts to the pan and cook for a minute or two until butter starts to brown, stirring constantly. Deglaze the pan with the lemon juice and as soon as the butter and lemon foams up and the tasty morsels on the pan loosen, pour the sauce over the walleye.

Lou Bignami
Moscow, Idaho

Walleye Baked with Sour Cream

This excellent German dish assembles easily, and you can cook it ahead of time, warm it in the oven, and then add and broil the sour cream topping on days when the cook is either busy or would rather spend time with guests. Try this dish with flavored rice or mashed potatoes.

    2 lbs. walleye fillets
    1 large red onion, sliced
    1 lemon, thinly sliced
    1 cup sour cream or yogurt for the diet folks
1-3 T. German mustard
    1 T. thyme
    ¼ cup seasoned bread crumbs
    2 T. or more of butter

Preheat oven to 350 degrees.

Butter a 9" x 13" baking dish and add fillets in a single layer. Salt and pepper the fillets and top with lemon slices. Cover the baking dish and bake about 25 minutes. Check for fish flaking at the thickest part of the fillet at 15 minutes as oven temperatures and cooking times vary.

While fish cooks beat mustard, thyme and sour cream. Toast bread crumbs with melted butter as needed.

When fish is done, remove lemon slices, turn on the broiler, spread sour cream on the fish and top with a mix of melted butter and seasoned bread crumbs. Set on the top rack under the broiler until coating is lightly browned. Serve at once.

Lou Bignami
Moscow, Idaho

Ten Minute Walleye Chowder

Walleye, like all tasty lean fish, makes wonderful chowder, soup, stew or bisques that are much improved if you use fish stock instead of water. You can also use powdered milk reconstituted with fish stock. If you don't make your own fish stock, you can substitute clam juice

This particular chowder uses clams, crabs, shrimp and whatever else you can find. We like it with crayfish instead of shrimp, mussels and various types of fresh clams instead of canned, and toss in whatever fish is handy. Combinations of fish, like walleye, salmon, catfish or yellow perch all work. Just keep the total amount the same.

1 lb. walleye, cooked and flaked	1 7½-oz. can of clams, minced
6 T. butter or margarine	3 cups fish stock or clam juice
(at room temperature)	½ cup white wine
1 onion, finely chopped	1 tsp. thyme
1 carrot, diced	1 tsp. dill
2 celery stalks, diced	3 T. flour
4 T. parsley	¼ tsp. salt
½ lb. cooked crab	½ tsp. white pepper
½ lb. shrimp or crayfish, shelled	
and cooked	

Melt 3 tablespoons of butter in a skillet over medium heat. Add onion, carrot, celery and parsley and saute until soft. Combine crab, walleye, shrimp, clams, fish stock or clam juice, wine, thyme and dill. Bring to a boil, reduce heat and simmer five minutes.

Mix flour and remaining butter into a ball.

Divide the seafood mixture in half. Put one half into a blender until smooth. Put the butter ball into the other half of the mix and cook over medium heat for about five minutes or until mixture thickens. Stir the blended mixture back into the pot. Bring the finished dish to serving temperature.

Lou Bignami
Moscow, Idaho

Walleye Curry Salad (aka Lou's Killer Walleye Sandwich Spread!)

Arguments rage.

She serves it with pineapple as a lady's luncheon salad on lettuce. He leaves out the pineapple, doubles the mayonnaise and uses it as a sandwich spread in a crusty French roll. Try it both ways.

- 1 cup cooked walleye, flaked
- 1 cup cooked shrimp, or crayfish
- 1 cup celery sliced into ¼-inch thick diagonals
- ¼ cup green onion tops chopped (he tosses in the whites, too)
- 2 T. lemon juice
- ½ cup water chestnuts, sliced
- 1 cup of pineapple chunks, drained
  salt and pepper to taste

Curry Dressing:

- ½ cup mayonnaise (more for sandwich spread as the bread will absorb some and tend to dry it out)
- ¼ cup sour cream or yogurt
- ¼-½ tsp. curry powder (depends on the type)

Mix the ingredients, toss with the dressing and serve.

Sandwich Tip #1: Make the spread but tote it to the water in the cooler and fill sandwiches on the spot. This keeps everything crisp and eliminates the chance of the filling going bad on a hot day.

Sandwich Tip #2: If you must make sandwiches early, "sandwich" the filling between lettuce leaves before you stick it in the sandwich and the result won't be soggy.

Lou Bignami
Moscow, Idaho

Melting Pot Walleye Cakes, Balls, Fingers, etc.

The basics of good fish cakes, fishballs, fish fingers or fish loaf is simple. Use soaked bread to keep things moist. This is vital with walleye and other lean fish that tend to be dry. We hope you make this dish with flakes from poached heads and backbones, but it also works with cooked fish.

Kids who don't usually eat fish will eat fish cakes served with a mayonnaise and pickle or mayonnaise-and-ketchup mix, a la the "Golden Arches." This is also an excellent dish to start kids cooking – small fry love squeezing wet bread!

2 cups cooked walleye, flaked	**1 tsp. Italian seasoning**
1 cup soaked stale bread	**1 T. olive oil**
1 egg	**2 T. grated Parmesan or**
¼ tsp. salt	**Romano cheese**
½ tsp. pepper	**3 T. dry bread crumbs**
2 T. parsley flakes	**6 T. vegetable oil**
1 tsp. basil	

Tear day-old bread into large pieces, cover with water and soak 10 minutes. Remove bread, squeeze out excess water. Combine fish, egg, salt, pepper, parsley, basil, Italian seasoning, olive oil, soaked bread and cheese in a bowl and mix well.

Form into cooking shapes: Golf ball sized pieces to make fishballs for pasta; patties allow ethnic variations and fish burgers. You can even make a fish loaf. If the mix is too soft to hold its shape add extra bread crumbs.

Heat oil and brown pieces nicely. Set cooked balls or pieces on paper towels until you gather buns and such.

- To got completely Italian, cook the fish balls in a meatless tomato sauce for about one hour and serve with pasta or use for fishball subs.
- To go French, cover the fish cakes with hollandaise or wine sauce.
- To go German, use cakes with a sour cream and mustard sauce.
- To go Polish, use a paprika and sour cream sauce.
- To go American, substitute fish cakes for cooked hamburger on buns.

Note: Both balls and pieces can be cooked ahead, immediately frozen on a greased cookie sheet and stored in sealed bags in the freezer until needed. They keep six months.

Lou Bignami
Moscow, Idaho

Goodies for
the Table

Fish Appetizer

1 lb. fresh water fish (crappie, bluegill, yellow perch, walleye, bass)
1 lemon, grated
½ cup salad dressing
1 T. (more more) horseradish
   salt and pepper to taste
1 T. onion, chopped fine
1 T. celery, chopped fine
1 T. cider vinegar
1 tsp. paprika

Poach fish in water until it flakes. Break up fine and remove any bones.

Wash fish under running water and scrub with lemon. Dry excess water with paper towel.

Add other ingredients to fish and mix well. Let set in refrigerator for 3-4 hours to blend flavors. Serve with crackers.

M. W. Jewell
W. Keansburg, New Jersey

Imitation Lobster Appetizer

   dolphin (dorado) cut in chunks
1 cup sugar
2 qt. water
   melted butter or cocktail sauce

Bring water and sugar to a boil. Drop in dolphin chunks and cook until fish floats to the surface. Serve with butter or cocktail sauce.

F. A. (Fritz) Backscheider
Batavia, Ohio

Seafood Omelet

2 T. green onions, chopped fine	1 tsp. white wine
1 T. butter	1 T. cream
6 oysters	1 T. canola oil
4 shrimp	3 eggs
2 T. crabmeat	dash Tabasco
4 mushrooms, fresh	salt and pepper to taste

Saute green onions in butter. Add oysters, shrimp, crabmeat, mushrooms, and wine. Cook until dry, then add cream.

Heat oil in omelet pan. Add eggs, seafood mixture and Tabasco. Season with salt and pepper and toss omelet until done.

Rene Broussard
New Iberia, Louisiana

Slimming Seafood Salad

1 lb. skinned fish fillets	1 sprig parsley
1 cup boiling water	½ bay leaf
1 T. lemon juice	salad greens
½ small onion, thinly sliced	garnish with: tomato wedges,
½ tsp. salt	cucumber slices, celery sticks,
2 peppercorns or dash of pepper	salad dressing, your choice

Place fish in well-greased frying pan. Add remaining ingredients except garnish and salad dressing. Cover and simmer 5-10 minutes or just until fish flakes easily when tested with a fork.

Carefully remove fish, drain, and place in covered dish in refrigerator to chill.

Arrange salad greens in bowl or on plate. Place tomato wedges, cucumber, and celery sticks around edge of greens. Heap chilled, poached fish in center. Serve with 1-2 tablespoons of your favorite salad dressing.

Evelyn Menli
Wrangell, Arkansas

Battered Fish

6-8 fresh fish fillets
1 cup flour
¾ cup cracker meal
1 tsp. garlic salt
1½ tsp. parsley
1 tsp. salt
1 tsp. pepper
2 eggs, beaten
½ stick margarine or butter

Shake all dry ingredients together in a bag. Dip fresh fish in eggs. Put fish in bag and shake until fish is well coated.

Fry fish in hot margarine or butter until golden brown.

Irene and Shawn Carr
New Brighton, Pennsylvania

Beer Batter DeBolt

1 cup plus 1 T. flour
salt
1 T. olive oil
¾ cup beer at room temperature
1 egg, separated

With a wire whisk, mix flour and a little salt. Add oil and beer and stir. Add egg yolk and whisk until blended. Cover mixing bowl with a clean cloth. Place in a warm location and let stand 2-3 hours.

Beat egg white until stiff. Fold into batter.

This can be used on fish, shrimp or vegetables. Fry at 375 degrees.

Dave DeBolt
Des Moines, Iowa

Beer Batter for Deep Frying

1½ cups flour
　1 tsp. baking powder
　½ tsp. salt
　1 T. white sugar
　1 cup beer
　1 egg, beaten

Mix flour, baking powder, salt and sugar. Add beer and egg. Dip fish in batter and deep fry. If you prefer a thinner batter, add more beer. Great on chicken, too.

Norma Blank
Shawano, Wisconsin

Beer Batter for Fish Fry

　2 cups flour
　2 tsp. baking powder
　2 tsp. salt to taste (about)
　　beer (about 4 cups)
　1 egg
　　dash of Worcestershire sauce

Mix flour, baking powder and salt. Add beer until thin enough to stick to fish. Add egg and Worcestershire sauce.

Coat fish and fry in deep fat.

This makes a large amount of batter. Cut recipe in half for smaller amount of fish.

Norma Blank
Shawano, Wisconsin

Cracker Battered Fillets

   1 lb. fish fillets, any kind
      lard, enough to fill pot 2 inches
   1 egg
   1 T. water
   1 cup crackers, crushed
   1 cup white flour
  ¾ tsp. salt
      pepper to taste
      seafood seasoning

Beat egg and add water. In a separate bowl, combine all other ingredients.

Dip fish fillets in egg mixture, then in cracker mixture. Deep fry until golden brown.

Benedict Miller
Dover, Delaware

Crispy Battered Fish

    1 lb. fish fillets, your choice
    1 cup all-purpose flour
    2 tsp. baking powder
  1¼ tsp. salt
    2 tsp. sugar
    1 T. olive oil
    1 cup beer (not light beer)

Mix dry ingredients. Add oil to beer. Make a well in dry ingredients and slowly pour in beer, stirring until well blended. Dip fish pieces in batter and deep fry or pan fry in oil until golden brown.

Sandy McKinnon
Ingleside, Ontario, Canada

Crispy & Spicy Beer Battered Fillets

1 lb. your favorite fish fillets
1 cup flour
1 T. cornmeal
½ tsp. white pepper
1 T. Cajun spices
¾ can beer

Blend all ingredients except fish thoroughly. Heat 1" of oil in skillet or fryer set at 375 degrees.

Dip fillets in batter and fry to a golden brown (about 2½ -3 minutes per side).

Scott Griffin
Isanti, Minnesota

Tim's Fish Batter

1 cup flour
1 tsp. salt
½ cup sugar
1 tsp. baking soda
1 egg
1 cup very cold water

Sift dry ingredients together. Beat egg until fluffy. Add dry ingredients to egg. Add water. Stir until thoroughly blended. Excellent for deep or pan frying.

Tim Kitowski
Stevens Point, Wisconsin

Grandma Vollmer's Beer Batter Fish

6-8 fish fillets
  1 egg
  ½ cup flour
  ½ can beer

Beat egg slightly. Add flour. Slowly add beer.

Dip fish in batter and deep fry until golden brown.

David K. Neff
Montpelier, Indiana

Jerry's Beer Batter

  1 lb. fish fillets
  ⅔ cups flour
  1 tsp. salt
  ½ tsp. baking powder
  ⅓ cup beer
  1 egg

Mix flour, salt, baking powder, beer and egg together and blend thoroughly. Dip fillets in batter and deep fry in hot oil until done.

Jerry Solberg
Weyauwega, Wisconsin

Tempura Batter

    1 cup flour
    ⅓ tsp. salt
    ⅓ tsp. pepper
    ⅓ tsp. onion salt
    1⅓ tsp. baking powder
    1 cup cold water
    1 egg, beaten

Mix dry ingredients. Add cold water and egg and blend until smooth. Dip fish, shrimp, mushrooms, chicken or vegetables in batter, then deep fry.

F. A. (Fritz) Backscheider
Batavia, Ohio

Don's Favorite Walleye Chowder

4 walleye, boned and cubed
10 medium potatoes
2 cloves garlic
¼ green pepper, minced

6 whole bay leaves
salt and pepper to taste
¼ lb. butter or margarine
1 can condensed milk

Peel and cube potatoes. Combine potatoes, garlic, green pepper, bay leaves and salt and pepper in a pot of water. Water should cover ⅓ of ingredients. Cook over medium heat. When potato is cooked, add walleye. Cook for 3-5 minutes. Add butter. Add condensed milk and heat through.

Don Held
Addison, Michigan

Classic Fish Chowder

1 lb. haddock, cod, perch or other
    firm-fleshed whitefish, gutted
3 cups water
½ cup apple juice
2 T. vegetable oil
¾ cup onion, diced
¼ cup celery, diced
¼ cup green pepper, diced

¼ cup carrots, diced
2 cups potatoes, diced
2 cups skim milk
2 T. fresh parsley, minced
2 T. fresh fennel, minced
1 tsp. lemon rind, minced
    paprika, chopped scallions and
        fresh parsley for garnish

Place fish in a large saucepan. Add water and apple juice and bring to a boil. Reduce heat, cover and simmer until fish is tender and flakes easily with a fork (10-15 minutes). Remove fish from stock and set both aside.

In a large soup pot, heat oil and saute onions, celery, green pepper and carrots until soft, about 5 minutes. Add potatoes and reserved stock, cover and bring to a boil. Reduce heat and simmer until potatoes are fork-tender, 30-45 minutes.

Remove any skin or bones from cooked fish. Then cut fish into 1" pieces and add to soup. Stir in milk. Top with minced parsley, fennel and lemon rind. Garnish each bowl of hot chowder with paprika, chopped scallions and parsley.

Leo G. J. Seffelaar
Broadview, Saskatchewan

Fish Chowder

2-4 cups cooked, flaked fish, with
      bones removed
6 medium potatoes, cut into cubes
1 cup carrots
⅓ cup onion, chopped
1 cup celery, chopped
1 can corn
1 T. salt

3 cups water
⅓ cup butter
½ tsp. Worcestershire sauce
⅓ cup white wine
¼ tsp. basil
¼ tsp. thyme
    salt and pepper to taste

Combine all ingredients in a dutch oven and simmer until potatoes are tender. Add milk if chowder becomes too thick.

Craig Finnesgard
Faribault, Minnesota

Jim's Favorite Chowder

3 pt. oysters, shucked
3 cups whole milk
1 cup heavy cream
4 medium red potatoes
½ cup bacon, chopped
½ cup onions, chopped
3 6½-oz. cans chopped clams

In a large pot over medium heat, combine milk and cream. Do not boil. Peel and dice potatoes and add to milk.

Chop bacon and fry until cooked, but not crispy. Add chopped onion to bacon and cook until tender. Remove bacon and onion from grease and add to milk.

Drain juice from oysters into a separate saucepan. Quarter oysters and dump them into their juice. Cook over medium heat until edges curl. Add oysters and juice into milk. Add clams and their juice to milk. Heat all ingredients thoroughly. When potatoes are done, chowder is ready to eat.

Jim and Erica Morris
Marysville, Washington

Oyster Gumbo

½ gal. oysters, freshly shucked
½ cup flour
¼ cup cooking oil
2 cups onions, chopped
1½ cups celery, chopped
¼ cup garlic, chopped

¼ cup parsley, chopped
¼ cup shallots, chopped
½ cup ground sassafras leaves
   (filé powder)
salt and pepper to taste

In a large pot, pour enough cooking oil to cover the bottom to about ⅛ inch. Place over low heat and stir in flour. Stir constantly until flour becomes a dark caramel color. This is a roux and is the basis for many Cajun dishes.

When the roux is the right color, add onions, celery and garlic. Stir constantly, adding a little warm water to avoid sticking until the onions and celery are soft.

Add the oysters and cook until the edges begin to curl. If you add the oyster liquid, cut down on additional salt. Add 2-3 quart warm water and simmer 30-45 minutes. Add parsley and shallots and cook for 5 more minutes. Turn off heat and add the sassafras leaves or filé powder. Stir until slightly thickens. Serve over cooked rice.

Tracy Lapeyrouse
Houma, Louisiana

Baked Fish in Sour Cream

3 lb. fish fillets, any kind
½ tsp. salt
¼ tsp. pepper

1 onion, sliced
1 cup thick sour cream
   watercress or other greens for garnish

Place fish in buttered or oiled flat baking dish. Sprinkle both sides of fish with salt and pepper. Let stand 10 minutes. Cover fish with onion slices.

Bake uncovered in 350-degree oven until fish flakes when tested with a fork (about 30-35 minutes). Baste fish with cream. If liquid evaporates too fast, add a little hot water.

Serve in same dish, garnished with watercress or any green garnish.

Jerry Solberg
Weyauwega, Wisconsin

Baked Lemon and Herb Fish

1-2 lb. fresh fish, filleted about ½ inch thick
¼ cup lemon juice
1 tsp. thyme
1 tsp. savory
  dash pepper
1 tsp. parsley
1 T. butter, cut into small pieces

Grease bottom of a glass baking dish and lay fish, skin-side down, in a single layer.

Sprinkle lemon juice and butter evenly over fish. Mix spices and herbs and evenly spread over fish.

Bake at 450 degrees for 10 minutes or until fish flakes with a fork.

Charles and Tamara Johnson
Albany, Oregon

Broiled Smelt

2 lbs. smelt
  oil
¼ cup butter, melted
  salt and pepper

Preheat oven to 550 degrees.

Lightly oil a shallow cookie sheet. Rinse smelt under cold water. Pat dry and lay out on cookie sheet. Place under broiler for 5 minutes.

Remove smelt from broiler and pour butter over top. Season with salt and pepper. Place smelt back under broiler for another 2-3 minutes or until golden brown.

Bryan Lasher
Union City, Pennsylvania

Chipper Cheese Fish

1 lb. fish fillets
3 T. melted butter
2 T. lemon juice concentrate
1½ cups potato chips, crushed
¼ cup Parmesan cheese, grated

Preheat oven to 350 degrees.

Pour butter into a greased 13" x 9" pan and stir in lemon juice. In a medium bowl, combine chips and cheese. Set aside.

Dip fish in butter and lemon mixture, then dip in chips and cheese mixture. Arrange in baking pan. Top with remaining chip mixture.

Bake 20-25 minutes or until fish flakes with a fork.

Sue Hilfinger
Davenport, Iowa

Easy Baked Fish

2 lbs. fish fillets
2 tomatoes
1 large onion, sliced
   salt and pepper to taste

Put fish in baking dish. Layer tomatoes and sliced onion on top. Add salt and pepper to taste.

Bake until fish flakes when tested with a fork.

Mary Plummer
LaVale, Maryland

Nautilus Fish Bake

  1 lb. fish fillets
  2 T. margarine
  ¼ cup celery, sliced
  ¼ cup onion, chopped
  2 T. margarine
  2 T. flour
  ¼ tsp. salt
  ¼ tsp. dillweed
  1 cup milk
  ½ cup Parmesan cheese, grated
  1 T. lemon juice

Saute vegetables in margarine. Blend in flour and seasonings. Gradually add milk while stirring.

Cook, stirring constantly, until sauce boils and thickens. Add cheese and lemon juice. Stir until well blended.

Place fish in 11" x 7" baking dish. Top with sauce. Bake at 350 degrees for about 25 minutes or until fish flakes easily with a fork.

Tim Kitowski
Stevens Point, Wisconsin

Oven-Baked Fish Fillets

  4 fish fillets
    salt and pepper
    lemon juice
  4 strips bacon

Sprinkle each fillet with salt, pepper, and lemon juice.

Wrap each fillet in a strip of bacon. Arrange on greased hot platter or shallow baking dish and bake at 350 degrees until fish flakes when tested with a fork (about 25 minutes).

Jerry Solberg
Weyauwega, Wisconsin

Oven-Fried Fish

1 lb. fish fillets, your favorite
2 T. cornmeal
2 T. dry bread crumbs
¼ tsp. salt
⅛ tsp. pepper

¼ tsp. paprika
⅛ tsp. dried dill weed
¼ cup milk
3 T. margarine, melted

Place oven rack in middle of oven. Pre-heat oven to 400 degrees.

Mix cornmeal, bread crumbs, salt, pepper, paprika, and dill weed. Dip fish into milk and then coat with cornmeal mixture.

Place coated fillets in a generously greased pan. Drizzle melted margarine over fish. Bake, uncovered, until fish flakes easily with a fork.

Samuel Gontkovsky
Davie, Florida

Oven-Fried Panfish

4 fish fillets
  cooking oil
1 egg

1 T. milk
2 cups seasoned bread crumbs
  seasonings to taste

Pre-heat oven to 450 degrees.

Pour a shallow layer of oil in a baking pan or cookie sheet; you need only enough to coat the fillets and keep them from sticking.

Beat egg with milk. Dip fillets in egg and roll in bread crumbs.

Place fillets in the oiled pan, turning once to coat both sides with oil. Bake 9-12 minutes, depending on thickness, turning over once half way through cooking.

You can add spices or seasonings to the bread crumbs to give the fish slightly different flavors. Try garlic salt, pepper or cayenne pepper. For another interesting variety, try one of the flavored cooking oils.

Allan Bockrath
Fort Leavenworth, Kansas

Spicy Baked Fish

4 fish fillets, your choice
  margarine
  salt and pepper to taste
  jalapeno pepper to taste
1 clove garlic, chopped

Cover sheets of aluminum foil (large enough to wrap each fillet) with margarine. Add salt and pepper over margarine. Lay fish on foil. Season to taste. Lay a sliced jalapeno pepper on top of each fillet, and sprinkle each with garlic.

Seal fish in foil. Bake at 350-400 degrees until flaky. Serve with rice.

Bryan Lasher
Union City, Pennsylvania

Spicy Baked Whitefish

1½ lbs. boned fillets of whitefish
 ½ lb. butter cut into pats
 ½ cup carrots, grated
 ¼ tsp. cayenne pepper
1½ tsp. garlic powder
  1 T. oregano
  1 T. Italian seasoning
1½ tsp. seasoned salt
  3 cups white rice, cooked

Preheat oven to 350 degrees.

In a 9" square glass baking dish, cover bottom with half the butter.

In separate dish, mix all the spices. Put half of this mixture over butter. Place fish on top. Cover with remaining butter, then remaining spices. Top with carrots.

Bake, uncovered, for 15-20 minutes. Serve over warm rice. Top with juice from dish.

Kat Wittlieff
Racine, Wisconsin

Stuffed Baked Redfish Casserole

    1 large or 2 small redfish, filleted
       wild rice mix
    1 pkg. bread stuffing
    ¼ cup crabmeat or shrimp (optional)
    ¼ cup mushrooms, sliced
    1 stick of butter or margarine
       lime juice
       salt and pepper
       other seasonings as desired (garlic, paprika, etc.)

Preheat oven to 375 degrees.

Cook wild rice. A mix can be substituded to save time. Clean and debone fillets.

In a large bowl, mix about half a package of bread stuffing according to package directions. Add crab or shrimp, if desired. Stir in rice, mushrooms and all other ingredients.

Grease a large baking dish and lay fish on bottom. Sprinkle lime juice over fish. Add salt and pepper to taste. Cover fillets with about half of the stuffing mixture, adding extra along the sides. Lay another layer of fish on top and finish off with stuffing. Dot butter on top and bake for 30-40 minutes. Test with fork for flakiness.

Great dish for people who haven't eaten fish before. Works well with most white, solid fish.

Bill Burrows
St. Petersburg, Florida

Tomato-Topped Fish

1½ lb. fish fillets
 2 T. lemon juice
1½ cups water
 2 T. lemon juice
   black pepper
 ½ green pepper, minced
2½ T. onion, minced
 2 tomatoes, sliced
 ½ cup bread crumbs
 1 T. oil
   basil

Mix lemon juice with water. Soak fillets in water-lemon mixture for 10-15 minutes, turning after half the time. Drain.

Place fish in greased baking dish. Season with pepper to taste.

Mix onion with green pepper and spread ¾ of mixture evenly over fish. Cover with tomato slices. Mix bread crumbs, oil and rest of onion mixture and spread over tomato and fish. Sprinkle with basil.

Bake 10-15 minutes at 350 degrees.

Shirley Waller
Heuvelton, New York

Crab-Potato Pancakes

1 cup crab meat	6 T. flour
1 large potato, grated	1 egg
1 small onion	1 tsp. baking powder
2 T. parsley	2 T. mayonnaise
½ tsp. oregano	1 cup crab meat

Mix all ingredients and roll into balls. Flatten each ball to make pancakes. Fry and serve.

Milton W. Jewell
W. Keansburg, New Jersey

Darrel's Smoked Fish

1 fish of your choice
 lemon pepper
 garlic powder
 dill
4 T. butter
1½ T. lemon juice

Trim spoonbill well. Sprinkle fish with seasonings and let stand 20 minutes.

Place fish on fish grate over hot coals or grill. Add a mixture of mesquite and alderwood chips to the coals as desired.

Mix lemon juice with butter and brush over fish. Cook fish 3-5 minutes per side, depending on thickness of fish. Turn carefully. Brush with lemon butter after turning.

If you don't have a fish grate, poke holes in heavy-duty aluminum foil and spray with nonstick cooking spray. Place fish on foil for cooking.

Darrel and Mary Ann Keller
Parsons, Kansas

Sauces and Marinades

Fish Marinade Grilling Sauce

¼ lb. margarine or butter
2 tsp. lemon juice
2 tsp. yellow mustard
6 tsp. brown sugar

1 tsp. onion salt
1 tsp. pepper
1 tsp. garlic salt
1 shot brandy (optional)

Bring butter, lemon juice and mustard to a boil. Remove from heat. Stir in brown sugar and keep stirring until syrupy. Add other spices and brandy, if desired. Brush on fish before and during grilling

Ruth Ann Donley
Mount Joy, Pennsylvania

Marinated Fish Fillets

2-3 lb. fish fillets (pan fish works well)
¾ cup low-salt soy sauce
1 tsp. ground ginger
2 cups yellow cornmeal

1 tsp. Morton's Season All
1 egg
½ cup warm beer
butter-flavored shortening for frying

Make the marinade by combining the soy sauce and ginger. Place fish in marinade and refrigerate 6-8 hours, stirring occasionally.

Combine cornmeal and Season All in a large resealable plastic bag and shake to mix.

In a small bowl, beat egg into beer. Dip fillets in egg mixture, shaking off the excess. Place fillets in bag containing cornmeal. Shake the bag to coat fillets evenly.

Heat enough butter-flavored shortening in the skillet until it is ¼" deep. Place fillets in skillet and fry for about 3 minutes on each side until browned. Fish should flake easily when tested with fork.

Remove fillets from skillet and place on paper towels to absorb excess oil.

Elvin M. Rose
Ransen, West Virginia

Mustard Sauce for Fish

3½ tsp. dry mustard
  1 cup mayonnaise
  2 tsp. Worcestershire sauce

1 tsp. A-1 sauce
⅛ cup whipping cream

Whisk everything together. Serve as a side sauce with your favorite fish or crab recipe.

Garnish with lemon wedges.

Dave DeBolt
Des Moines, Iowa

Fish Story and Recipe

1 fish, whole
1 onion
1 clove garlic

1 lemon
1 stick salt margarine

For 26 years, I was an over-the-road trucker. When I went on a trip, I always took my rod, reel and tackle box with me. In July 1973, I had to drive from Endicott, New York to Victoria, British Columbia, with stops in Moscow, Idaho, and Columbia Falls, Montana.

After these deliveries, I headed south, up the Clear Water River. I was tired, so I pulled over for the night. I found a wide spot on the side of the road, parked, and took out my rod and reel. I put a fly on the line, cast out into the river and BAM, I had a strike.

And what a strike. It was a solid 5 pound trout. I quickly cleaned the fish, built a fire and then went to my trailer and got my cooler. All I had in it was a small yellow onion, a clove of garlic, one lemon and a stick of margarine. No real food! So I got out some foil, put the fish on it, along with onion, sliced, and lemon cut in slices—and, of course, not to forget the garlic. I then put some margarine and a little salt on the fish, wrapped it in foil and put it in the coals.

After cooking, I opened the foil package up and what an aroma! Boy, was I hungry. It was great, too. So every time I go fishing, I take my cooler and all the same ingredients with me. That's my story, and I'm sticking to it.

Jerry Fannin
North East Salem, Oregon

The recipes that fill the rest of this section were provided by Lawry's Foods for the enjoyment of NAFC Members. They are all camp and kitchen tested by Lawwry's staff of outdoor writers, chefs and sportsmen.

Quick N' Easy Microwave Fish Fillets

1 lb. boneless fillets of bass, walleye or crappie
1 12-oz. bottle Lawry's Herb & Garlic with Lemon Juice Marinade
   Lawry's Lemon Pepper
   Lawry's Seasoned Salt

In a sealable plastic bag or glass bowl, combine fillets and Lawry's Herb and Garlic marinade, reserving ¼ cup. Refrigerate for at least 30 minutes (overnight is o.k.). Remove fillets, let drain and arrange in a single layer in a glass baking dish. Add ¼ cup marinade and sprinkle with Lawry's lemon pepper and seasoned salt. Microwave on high for 5-7 minutes, or until fillets flake easily. Serve with slaw and corn on the cob.

Ann's Baked Crappie

2 lbs. crappie fillets (or walleye, or bass)
1 green bell pepper
   flour
   Parmesan or Monterey Jack cheese
   butter
   Lawry's Garlic Pepper
   Lawry's Seasoned Salt
   Lawry's Seasoned Pepper

In a skillet, heat butter. Combine flour and Lawry's Garlic Pepper and dredge fillets. Brown the fillets in butter and arrange in a single layer in a glass baking dish (buttered). Cut green pepper into pieces and puree in blender or food processor. Make a white sauce (butter, flour and milk) and melt cheese into it (½ cup Parmesan or 1 cup Monterey Jack), blend well and add pureed bell pepper. Sprinkle with Lawry's Seasoned Pepper and pour over fish. Bake at 350 degrees for approximately 20 minutes. Serve over a bed of white rice.

Breakfast (Or Anytime) Trout

This is a quick, no fuss breakfast treat. You can fix it at home but it works well in a cabin, an RV parked beside the water, or, best of all, eaten balanced on one knee around a campfire on the banks of a trout stream. It's also delicious as lunch or a light supper.

> **pan-sized trout, head and tail attached, 1 or 2 per person**
> **butter, margarine or oil**
> **croutons or cut up toast**
> **flour**
> **Lawry's Seasoned Salt & Lawry's Lemon Pepper**

Other ingredients you have on hand–use your imagination: diced onions, celery, bell peppers, green chilies, mushrooms, leftover steak, ham or chicken, bacon bits, peas, corn, etc. Be creative.

Sauté the veggies and/or meat, cut into small pieces. Shake the trout in a paper bag with generous amounts of Lowary's Seasoned Salt and Lemon Pepper, then in a separate pan, fry in butter or oil. When you turn the trout, add the ingredients from the other pan and when ready to serve, lightly stuff the trout with the veggie/meat mixture and heap more on top.

Lemon Pepper Baked Trout Or Salmon

1 trout or salmon (big enough to stuff), deboned
2 small cans crab meat
2 small cans shrimp pieces
½ cup celery, diced
1 medium tomato, chopped
1 12 oz. bottle Lawry's Lemon Pepper with Lemon Juice Marinade
  Lawry's Lemon Pepper
  Lawry's Seasoned Salt

To debone the fish, clean, leaving the head, tail and fins attached. Lay the fish on its back and insert a sharp, thin-bladed knife just under the rib bones. Cut up toward the belly of the fish, freeing the ribs. Work both sides, then cut around the backbone and remove the complete skeleton. Do not cut into the back meat or skin.

Place the fish in a plastic bag, add the bottle of Lawry's Lemon Pepper Marinade and refrigerate for at least two hours. Remove and drain.

Mix the crab and shrimp with the diced celery and tomato and stuff the fish. Tie with string and place in a covered roaster or make a "tent" of tightly sealed foil. Bake at 350 degrees for 15 minutes per pound. When the fish is done, remove to a heated platter, cut the string and slide off the skin. Let the individual eaters add Lawry's lemon pepper and seasoned salt to taste.

Lemon Pepper Fish Fillets

fillets for four—bass, crappie, walleye, perch, etc.
1 12 oz. bottle Lawry's Lemon Pepper with Lemon Juice Marinade
fine bread crumbs (seasoned or plain)
2 T. butter or margarine
2 T. salad oil
⅓ cup light cream or half-and-half
1 tsp. fresh grated lemon peel
Lawry's Seasoned Salt
Lawry's Lemon Pepper
sliced almonds

In a resealable plastic bag, combine fillets and Lawry's Lemon Pepper marinade and refrigerate for two hours. Remove fillets, add Lawry's Seasoned Salt and Lemon Pepper and roll in bread crumbs. Mix oil and butter/margarine in a skillet and saute' fillets for 3-4 minutes on each side–or until golden brown and fish flakes easily. Remove to a serving platter and keep warm. Add the cream and grated lemon peel to the pan drippings and bring to a boil, stirring constantly until slightly thickened. Spoon over fillets and sprinkle with sliced almonds.

Teriyaki Bass (Or Walleye, Crappie, Etc.) Fillets

2 lbs. boneless fish fillets
¼ cup dry sherry
1 large tomato, diced
2 T. orange juice
1 T. Dijon-style mustard
½ cup thinly sliced green onion
1 12 oz. bottle Lawry's Teriyaki Marinade with Pineapple Juice

In a bowl, combine Teriyaki marinade with Pineapple Juice, sherry, orange juice and mustard and mix with wire whisk. Add fillets and refrigerate for one to two hours, turning occasionally. In a small bowl, combine tomato and onion and set aside. Remove fillets, reserving marinade. Broil or grill 3-5 minutes, brushing once with marinade. Turn, spoon vegetables over fillets and cook until fish flakes easily. Serves four.

Run For The Border Fish Fillets

1 pound walleye, bass, crappie or other white fish fillets
1 package (1.25 ounces) Lawry's Taco Spices & Seasoning
¾ tsp. Lawry's Garlic Powder with Parsley
½ tsp. Lawry's Seasoned Pepper
2 T. butter or margarine
  lemon wedges

In a shallow dish, combine flour, Taco Spices & Seasonings, Garlic Powder with Parsley and Seasoned Pepper. Rinse fish, pat dry with paper towels. Coat both sides of fish with flour mixture. In a large, non-stick skillet, melt butter. Add fish, cook 5 minutes on each side or until fish flakes easily. Squeeze lemon wedges over fish when serving.

Easy Fish Gumbo

This is a stick-to-the-ribs fare, good anytime, but most appreciated when it's cold outside and you want to get warm inside. Use any kind of fish, from crappies to carp.

1½ lbs. fish, cut in bite-sized pieces
¾ cup celery, diced
¾ cup green bell pepper, diced
¾ cup onion, diced
1 clove garlic, finely chopped
3 T. olive oil
1 pound can tomatoes and juice
2 cups cooked rice
1 12-16 oz. pkg frozen okra
1 bay leaf
½ tsp. thyme

3 beef bouillon cubes
½ tsp. Lawry's Seasoned Pepper
3 cups boiling water
2½ T. Lawry's Seasoned Salt

Sauté celery, pepper, onion and garlic in oil. In a pot, dissolve the bouillon cubes in boiling water and add tomatoes, okra, sautèed veggies and seasonings. Cover and simmer for 30 minutes. Add fish and simmer an additional 20 minutes; use tomato juice to thin if desired. Sprinkle with filè or hot sauce to taste and serve in bowls over cooked rice.

No Guilt Baked Fish Fillets In Sour Cream

Use crappie, bass, walleye, perch or any white-flashed salt water species and don't–as in do not–count calories. Don't worry about guilt, just enjoy an easy-to-fix, delicious dish.

2 lbs. fish fillets
1½ cups sour cream
1 12 oz. bottle Lawry's Herb & Garlic
    Marinade with Lemon Juice
¾ cup real mayonnaise

¾ cup onion, finely chopped
Lawry's Seasoned Salt, to taste
dash of paprika

Put the fillets in a bowl or resealable plastic bag and add the Lawry's Herb & Garlic marinade; refrigerate for at least two hours (overnight is o.k.). Remove and drain, pat excess marinade from the fillets with a paper towel, then roll them in flavored bread crumbs, Italian works very well. Arrange the fillets in a single layer in a lightly buttered baking dish and sprinkle with Lawry's Seasoned Salt. Combine sour cream, onion and mayonnaise and cover fish with a thick layer of the mixture. Sprinkle with paprika and bake at 500 degrees for 15-20 minutes, or until light brown and bubbly.

Herb & Garlic Fish Fillets

fillets for four—bass, crappie,
    walleye, perch, etc.
1 5-oz. Foil Pack Lawry's Herb &
    Garlic with Lemon Juice
    Marinade
fine bread crumbs—seasoned
    or plain
2 T. butter or margarine

2 T. salad oil
⅓ cup light cram or half-and-half
1 tsp. fresh grated lemon peel
Lawry's Seasoned Salt
Lawry's Lemon Pepper
sliced almonds

In a resealable plastic bag, combine fillets and Lawry's Herb and Garlic marinade and refrigerate for two hours. Remove fillets, add Lawry's Seasoned Salt and Lemon Pepper and roll in bread crumbs. Mix oil and butter/margarine in a skillet and sauté fillets for 3-4 minutes on each side–or until golden brown and fish flakes easily. Remove to a serving platter and keep warm. Add the cream and grated lemon peel to the pan drippings and bring to a boil, stirring constantly until slightly thickened. Spoon over fillets and sprinkle with sliced almonds.

Stuffed Trout On The Grill

This recipe is good anytime, but best if the trout are cooked and eaten (preferably outdoors) the same day they come from the stream or lake. Clean the fish, leaving the head and tail attached.

> 1 10"-12" trout—one per person
>   Salad croutons
>   Lawry's Lemon Pepper
> 1 lime
> 1 5-oz. foil pack Lawry's Mesquite Marinade with Lime Juice

In a resealable plastic bag or bowl, combine the trout with Mesquite marinade (reserving one tablespoon) and refrigerate (or put in ice chest) for one hour. Remove, drain and sprinkle with Lawry's Lemon Pepper inside and out.

Break the croutons into smaller pieces, toss them with the remaining marinade and lightly stuff the trout, so the body cavity remains more or less closed. Slice the lime into thin slices and add a half-slice, minced, to the dressing in each fish. Grill over coals for approximately 15 minutes, turning once. Serve with slices of lime.

Index